Grass Roots Government

The County in American Politics

Susan Walker Torrence

Grass Roots Government

The County in American Politics

Robert B. Luce, Inc.   Washington-New York

Contents

To Ron

You must, therefore, descend by turns to dwell with the rest of the city, and must be accustomed to see the dark objects; for when you are accustomed you will be able to see a thousand times better than those who dwell there, and you will know what each of the images is, and of what it is an image, because you have seen the truth of what is beautiful and just and good. And so your city will become a waking reality, and not a dream like most existing cities, which are peopled by men fighting about shadows and quarrelling for office as though that were a notable good. . .

The Republic, Book VII.

Foreword

Most Americans live in a county. Whether or not this is one of the blessings of our democracy or one of the inherited burdens we must carry will be debated for the rest of this century.

Those of us whose deepest interest is in making the traditional American federal system work well for today and better for tomorrow must all agree that strong and effective local government is an absolute essential of a satisfactorily operating federalism. For millions who live outside cities, the county is the only general local government they know—and for millions who live inside cities, the county is increasingly important but still properly characterized as "that other government we also have."

The role of the county in the next decade can be crucial. In some areas it may be the vehicle for an emerging local government of the future—in other areas the county may not live up to this challenge and in some, the county may not even recognize the challenge.

Whatever the future significance of the county in the American governmental scheme may be, one thing is sure. Too little is known about the American county. It has been studied too little and too little has been written about it.

This unfortunate situation makes "Grass Roots Government" a most welcome publication. At last there is a description of the American county, its trials, its tribulations and its occasional triumphs. This book is a sympathetic and informed general guide to county government. However, it has enough real substance to be a valuable text in local government courses in our educational institutions.

Reading this book will give you an appreciation of the dream for the American county future which is the goal of the National Association of Counties. Whether or not you share this dream, you will have a basic knowledge of the American county which has not been available before.

"Grass Roots Government" can only serve to improve the chances for the future success of the American county and to strengthen American federalism by indicating the opportunities yet available to this lesser known level of American government.

Wm. R. MacDougall

Executive Director
Advisory Commission
on Intergovernmental
Relations

1. The County, Yesterday and Today

Getting to Know the County

Helen Treadmore glared from her living room window at the rezoning sign across the street. Damn! Damn! Damn! She shook her fist at it, as if that would do any good. She'd known this was serious business ever since she'd heard that Smith and Crutcheon, the developers, had been sneaking around buying up the lovely wooded property over there. So many peaceful years when the kids played along the paths all over that block. Now it was zoned for apartments...high rise apartments!

She wanted to cry, in fact she did. Her husband was district sales manager so he was away too much to look into it; she had to fight the battle alone. The value of the nice four-bedroom house they'd been paying the mortgage on for ten years was at stake. But what was she to do now? It seemed she'd called every office in the county, and what did she know about the county for heaven's sake? For years it had just been the place where the Treadmores and their neighbors lived. No sir... now she knew better; the county controlled these things, controlled their destiny.

When she'd found out the county was responsible, she was immediately at the phone, ready to call and make a fight of it; but what were the names of the commissioners? The

1

county switchboard operator referred her to information which referred her to public relations. George Swenzel was the commissioner from her district... she'd even voted for him, she'd remembered suddenly. Little good it did her when she called to find out he was in his courthouse office only one afternoon a week or, on being referred to his business office, when she learned he couldn't be reached there either.

On with the show, she'd said with determination... at first. She launched a search to find out which county department was responsible for this mess. The sign said rezoning application number X-346P, so she called the licenses and permits office; it seemed logical. Only partly so... they just issued the damn things, somebody else approved them. Try the zoning department, it was helpfully suggested. Well, they did authorize the licenses and permits office to issue, but they didn't actually approve the rezoning. With a sigh Helen turned from the window, moved to the couch where she plumped down to rest her head in her hand. On to the zoning board where, yes, they had recommended approval, though they didn't have final authority. Who was the commissioner from her district? Oh yes, she should call Mr. Swenzel; the commissioners had final authority in these matters.

Helen slouched further down in the couch, legs stretched out in front of her the way she did when she was a kid. Who would have thought this could happen? All the time she'd thought counties took care of welfare cases; now she finds out they have the power to ruin her lifetime investment. She glanced over at the phone... she was going to call her neighbors, by god! With signs and placards, they'd take to the streets.

The Importance of County Government

If you live in any state except Connecticut or Rhode Island, you might someday come to the shocking realization

—as Helen Treadmore did—that your life is vitally affected by your county government. Counties are the most widespread form of local government in the United States. With minor exceptions all 50 states, except Rhode Island and Connecticut,* are divided into counties. Today there are more than 3000 counties providing services and regulating the lives of 93 percent of America's people.

Counties are among the oldest governments, predating many states and most cities. Early English settlers arrived with this concept of local government which had been developing in England for about 1000 years. Despite the ensuing history of counties in America, the average citizen is not fully aware of what they do or why they exist. Historically citizens have identified with cities, not counties. The city government put in the traffic lights, picked up the trash, operated the hospital, policed the streets and ran the summer recreation programs. The mayor worked hand in hand with the chamber of commerce to bring the new factory to town, and the mayor cut the ribbon on the door once the factory was built. Counties, on the other hand, catered to the farmers, built the country roads and took care of the needy. For the increasingly urbanized citizen counties appeared to be of little concern. Who cared as long as daily life ran smoothly? Of course, some events focused attention on counties, such as an election every two to four years. Even then, many had only a vague notion of who the candidates were and what they stood for.

As times and needs change, so do governments and citizens. Today we are told that cities are bankrupt. Many reformers now tout counties as the local governments of the future. Why the switch? What is so great about counties? Can they deliver? Such are the legitimate concerns of citizens who are becoming disillusioned with government at all levels and who are making it their business to know what government

---

*Counties were abolished in these two states and their functions were assumed by the state governments.

does and how it does it. But a look at county government today may lead to something like Helen Treadmore's shock at finding out how far-reaching it is. In other cases it may cause disappointment that it so nearly resembles the county described in the junior high civics course, or it may arouse mild surprise and guarded optimism at its ability to handle contemporary problems. The truth is that there are over 3000 counties and each is different. Yet there are striking similarities: they operate under many of the same restraints, face many of the same opportunities and are being transformed by many of the same pressures. To the citizen who wants a better perspective on county government today—what it does, how it does it, and most importantly, what he can do about it — the following pages are dedicated.

The Basic Principles of County Government

There are three important factors to keep in mind about county government.

1. Counties are a part of the total American government system; their behavior is conditioned by what state governments have done and are doing and to a lesser degree by the federal government.
2. The changes and the proposals for modernization of recent years need to be seen in relation to the broader changes in society. The most profound of these is the mass movement to urban areas which has resulted in densely populated, metropolitan complexes.
3. The primary responsibilities of counties, as well as other governments, are to provide public goods and services and to regulate public behavior. However, their essential role would be overlooked if one did not realize that the process of deciding what goods and services should be provided and what and how

4

behavior should be regulated is a political one. All those involved in the county process—county officials and employees, special interests, citizens—are involved in politics.

It is easy enough to state basic principles, but another matter to describe in practical terms how these principles operate, let alone observe them in one's own county. All the principles are intertwined. Furthermore, they contain contradictory elements. For example, state governments place restrictions on county actions, but counties have room to maneuver and can, if they want to, bend the state rules to suit their needs. Many of the contradictions can be explained by history. Counties have been around since before the beginning of the nation. Though in some ways they do not seem to have changed in 300 years, in other ways they are up to date, even ahead of the times. They are a hodgepodge of the old and the new, of the tradition dating to early England and of contemporary America.

The State and County Relationship

Counties are the legal children of state governments, and many states treat them as irresponsible juveniles. States established counties and states can abolish them, as Connecticut did in 1960. State constitutions, most of them written in the late 18th and early 19th centuries, set forth the basic purposes of counties. Primarily they were to be a local branch of the state government responsible for implementing state policy, and secondarily a provider of assistance to local residents, especially in rural areas. Counties were not supposed to have a close relationship with citizens, define their needs or develop programs to serve them. This function was assigned to cities, which were given the responsibility to deliver the services needed by urban citizens.

Counties were supposed to keep the peace and do the

paperwork. Most states made counties responsible for maintaining law and order, jailing offenders and bringing them to trial; issuing marriage licenses, recording deeds, and taking care of other legal papers; collecting taxes, and supervising elections; and implementing the state's health and welfare assistance programs. In some states, counties were supposed to operate the schools. A few tasks were thrown in as direct services to constituents, such as building roads and giving advice on agricultural matters.

The role of counties influenced their boundaries. Entire states were divided arbitrarily so state policy could be implemented everywhere. As one can see on the maps of many states, especially in the Great Plains and the West, counties are shaped like rectangles or squares, although some have one squiggled side where the boundaries yielded to rivers, mountains, and the like. The county map of Kansas, for example, shows a state divided into 105 small squares. Early county boundaries bore little relationship to the settlement of people, except that each one was small enough for every citizen to reach the county courthouse in a day by horse. City boundaries, by contrast, were clearly related to settlements of people.

The position of counties as local overseers of state programs, as set forth in state constitutions and reinforced by boundary lines, was further clarified by the courts through the years. Two decisions were basic:

In 1854 U.S. Chief Justice Taney wrote, "The several counties are nothing more than certain portions of the territory into which the state is divided for more convenient exercise of the powers of [state] government."[1]
In 1857 the Ohio Supreme Court spelled out the difference between cities and counties, "A municipal corporation proper is created mainly for the interest, advantage and convenience of the locality and its people; a county organization is created almost exclusively with a view to the policy of the state at large, for the purposes of

6

political organization and civil administration... With scarcely an exception, all the powers and functions of the county organization have a direct and exclusive reference to the general policy of the state, and are, in fact but a branch of the general administration of that policy."[2]

In 1872 Iowa Judge John F. Dillon summarized the legal powers of counties in his *Commentaries on the Law of Municipal Corporations,* and made clear that plenary power resided with the state government and that the county government possessed only powers expressly granted them, necessarily implied or essential to the local government. His concept of the powers of the county was accepted nationwide. This narrow interpretation of county authority, known as "Dillon's Rule," discouraged counties from attempting to take on new responsibilities and strengthened the hand of state legislators over county matters. Dillon's Rule is operative today in more than half of the states, although legislatures in other states are rewriting constitutions and statutes to give counties more flexibility.

Organization of County Government

State governments not only kept tight reins on what counties could do, they also determined how they would be organized. Because counties were considered administrative and service branches of the state, it was logical for state governments to specify what their governing bodies would be called and how they should be structured. This marks another distinction between cities and counties: state constitutions and laws have very little to say about the organization of cities on the theory that these units were set up mainly to meet local needs, not state ones, and local residents should decide how to structure their own government.

The names given to county governing bodies vary from state to state. In Delaware, the governing body of Sussex

7

County is called the levy court; in Louisiana, the boards are called police juries, parish councils or commission councils; in Alaska they are named borough assemblies, and in West Virginia, they are the county courts. The most common name is board of county commissioners. Governing bodies vary in size, from the 34 counties in Georgia governed by one official to Pulaski County, Arkansas governed by a board of over 100 people. The national average is three to five commissioners.

Constitutions or laws in 17 states require that all counties be governed by a commission elected to handle both legislative and administrative business. Eighty-seven percent of all counties in the nation operate under this type of governing structure. Other states give counties more options: they may be governed by commissions or they may organize the governing authority in other ways, but sometimes the states describe the options in detail. More than half the states allow county commissioners to hire professional managerial help, and today about ten percent have a county manager (called chief administrative officer, county administrator, appointed county executive or other similar titles).[3] Under this setup, commissioners still exercise legislative and administrative authority, but they are relieved by the manager of the routine, day-to-day tasks of running the county. The authority granted to county managers varies. The more powerful can hire, fire, or suspend county employees, recommend policies and propose legislation to the governing board, and prepare budgets. The less powerful act as administrative assistants to the commission, which continues to supervise employees directly.

Today, 19 states are relinquishing their tight control, permitting some or all counties to adopt locally initiated charters. Sixty-one counties and combined city-counties now have charters, and 36 of these are governed by the elected executive-council form of government (with the executive performing the functions of a city mayor).[4] Administrative and executive powers are fairly centralized in the elected executive, who serves as the ceremonial and symbolic head of the county as well. Most executives develop a legislative program, both an operating and a capital budget to carry out their ideas, and take charge of administering the county. They are empowered to hire department heads and staff members.

The council is the legislative arm, and serves as a watchful critic when the executive office is controlled by a political party or faction other than that which dominates the legislature. Councils enact ordinances and resolutions, adopt budgets and establish tax rates, and usually are responsible for making zoning decisions.

Commissioners or council members and executives are responsible for handling general business, but they share specific responsibilities with a sizeable number of other elected officials required by the states. The sheriff, treasurer, attorney or solicitor, assessor, auditor, recorder or clerk, coroner, and judicial officers, are all elected and carry out state policy in their particular area independently of the governing council. These "row officers," as they are commonly called because the offices appear in a long row on county election ballots, are responsible to the electorate and to their superiors in state government. County officers cannot interfere, except to cut off or limit their budget appropriations.

States control counties not only by providing for their structure and enumerating their functions but by limiting the money they can raise to perform these functions, primarily in three ways. First, they stipulate the sources of county taxes, second, they limit the tax rate, and third, they limit the amount of indebtedness the county can incur. Many states also set maximum rates for property taxes which are allocated for specific purposes, such as roads, public buildings and so forth. This earmarking of funds often makes county budgeting difficult and confusing. Property taxes are the major source of county funds, accounting for more than 42 percent of general revenue raised in 1967, the latest year for which national figures are available.[5] This raises serious

9

problems of equity and of administration (see Chapter 3). Property taxes are not levied in accord with a person's ability to pay, nor is the amount a citizen pays necessarily related to the cost of county services he receives. Tax assessing procedures are often out of date and unfair. Furthermore, during times of inflation when the county must pay the going rate for goods, equipment, and employees to carry out its functions, the yield from the property tax does not keep pace unless an alert, ambitious assessor, immune from political pressures, constantly readjusts property values, or the commissioners take chances with reelection and increase the tax rate. On the other hand, during recessions the property tax yield remains fairly stable, preserving the county's ability to pay its bills.

States give counties money through grant programs and revenue sharing. In 1967, 40 percent of all county revenue came either from the state or the federal government, with the state providing the lion's share.[6] Some of this money is earmarked, but much of it can be spent in any way the county sees fit.

The history of strong state control over local affairs has led, generally, to meek county governments, reluctant to experiment and reticent to press for more authority. Though many officials are willing to let things ride and to continue plugging along in the established ways, this is not universally true. Many have willingly exercised authority, in some cases even overstepping the restrictions of the state, while others have kept pace with the times because their constituents have demanded it.

Urbanization and the Contemporary County

Despite the many weaknesses of county governments, reformers are suggesting that counties may be the government of the future, especially for urban areas. Some even imply that the county is the only local government which will be capable of handling 21st century local problems. This is because 70 percent of the nation's citizens now live in urban areas, and counties, thanks to their large geographic bases, have the potential for handling areawide programs, delivering and financing areawide services, and coordinating those programs of smaller governments which affect the entire region. In most cases counties are the largest geographic jurisdiction in urban areas, with a few exceptions such as New York City, which consists of five boroughs or counties, and Boston which includes more than one county. About half of the 267 Standard Metropolitan Statistical Areas (SMSAs)* in the United States consist of a single county, and in many of the others the central county takes in well over 50 percent of the area population.

Counties have always had large territorial bases, but this attribute has been appreciated only recently as criticism of the way metropolitan areas are governed continues to mount and effective solutions become more elusive. Many political scientists, practical politicians and citizens complain that urban areas are not being governed effectively, mainly because no single general purpose government has emerged as a leader. To date both cities and counties have been unable to exert this leadership: cities have had the authority to furnish the necessary services but have been prevented from acquiring an areawide geographic base; counties have had the territorial jurisdiction, but have not had the authority to offer a wide range of functions.

During the early years of urbanization, until the 1900s, cities generally assumed the lead. They exercised their powers

---

*Standard Metropolitan Statistical Areas, defined by the U.S. Census Bureau as a county or group of adjacent counties containing at least one central city of 50,000 or twin cities with a combined population of 50,000, plus other adjacent counties which are essentially metropolitan in character.

to provide urban services and took advantage of liberal state annexation laws to enlarge their boundaries as adjacent territory was developed. After 1900 and for the next 45 to 50 years, central cities had difficulty maintaining their dominant positions as state legislatures passed stiff requirements to prevent further enlargement of the central city and made incorporation of new municipalities easier. In many states, new towns could become legal entities with as few as 100 residents. In fact before 1949 a group of 25 freeholders and registered voters could set up a municipal corporation in Dade County, Florida.[7] Politics accounted for the change in state attitudes. Most state legislatures were dominated by representatives from rural and urbanizing areas who did not want to risk losing their power to representatives of central cities. The actions of the legislatures reflected the attitudes of suburban residents toward the central city, also. As central cities began to show signs of age and deterioration, to become inhabited by "undesirable" residents, and to raise their tax rates, suburbanites preferred to divorce themselves from these problems by setting up new municipal corporations. As a result, central cities were surrounded by numerous small, autonomous towns.

Suburbanites not wanting to be a part of the central city had few viable alternatives, mainly because counties in most states did not have the powers to offer urban services they needed or to safeguard their autonomy from the city. Except in California, Maryland, Virginia and a few other states, counties could not provide fire protection, garbage pickup and other essentials. Even so, suburbanites not wanting to establish new cities could have chosen to live in the unincorporated county and set up special districts to supply municipal services. Many have preferred this arrangement; in 1970 nearly ten million urbanites lived in unincorporated areas.[8] However, in most states, unincorporated communities had one serious drawback from the suburbanites' point of view: despite the rigid laws, these communities were vulnerable to annexation by their municipal neighbors.

Perhaps worst of all, suburbanites of unincorporated communities had little control over the zoning and subdivision of nearby land because their counties either lacked zoning authority or were not always aggressive in exercising it, while municipalities often had the power to zone for limited distances beyond their borders.

Political maps of most metropolitan areas reflect these forces. Usually one or more counties encompass a central city surrounded by innumerable small towns, all of which is further complicated by additional divisions into special districts and school districts. As of June 1972 there were about 21,266 local governments—counties, municipalities, special districts and school districts—in urban areas, an average of 80 per metropolitan area.[9]

Most of these jurisdictions have their own elections and operate autonomously, often with little concern for what happens next door. Urban areas are socially and economically integrated but separated politically. The indictments of this system are many:

Urban areas are not governed democratically. Decisions made by one town affect residents of the entire area who have no voice in the decision.

Public services for urban areas are not financed democratically. Urban areas are socioeconomic complexes. Residents of one town work in another town, attend the theater in a third town, and go to church in a fourth. They use the entire area, place burdens on all the governments and therefore should help pay the cost of public services for the entire area. But they don't. They pay for their city and county only.

The fragmented governmental system of urban areas is impractical. Individually, the small jurisdictions cannot handle areawide problems such as air and water pollution. Furthermore, it is inefficient and a waste of money for each jurisdiction to provide a full complement of municipal services. A combined operation would be

13

less costly per capita and probably could attract a more professional staff.

As a result critics of urban government often turn to counties simply because they cover a lot of ground, which is one basis for rectifying many of the problems. Attempting to create regional governments (by merging the central city and county or by other means) have generally met with defeat at the polls. Many who would reform urban areas believe counties offer the most politically feasible way to come to grips with pressing public service needs, if only all of them could be equipped with up-to-date organizational structures, broader functional authority, and more effective fiscal powers. However, the states determine to what extent counties can reorganize, deliver services, and raise money. Proposals to reform counties must be directed toward the states, and several suggestions have been made on how state legislatures can strengthen counties. Those issued by the U.S. Advisory Commission on Intergovernmental Relations (ACIR) in 1971 are typical:

Give counties more flexibility in organizing their governing bodies and administrative departments by:
— authorizing them to adopt the one of several optional forms of government most suited to the individual county's needs
— authorizing counties to consolidate, if approved by popular referendum.
Give counties more flexibility to respond to constituent needs by:
— allowing them to assume responsibility for functions currently handled by municipalities
— allowing them to perform, on their own initiative, functions and services of a municipal character throughout all or part of their jurisdictions, even though not specifically authorized by the state
— allowing them to exercise joint powers with other

14

governments through agreements and contracts — allowing them to offer a broader range of services on an areawide basis.

Give counties more authority to govern metropolitan areas by:
— increasing their power to supervise special districts
— authorizing them to review and approve certain planning and zoning actions of cities
— empowering them to establish a joint local agency of elected city and county leaders to review petitions for incorporation of and annexation to cities, and for the creation, reorganization, consolidation or dissolution of special service districts.

Give counties more financial flexibility by allowing them to set up a subordinate taxing and service area for residents who want additional county services. To this suggestion for financial reform the National Association of Counties (NACO) would add: remove restrictions limiting county debt based on the local property tax and remove the requirement that all bond issues be subject to popular referendum.[10]

Some states have responded in part to the advice of the Advisory Commission on Intergovernmental Relations and the National Association of Counties with the result that some of their counties, both urban and rural, have completely reorganized or have developed innovative approaches to providing services. Great progress has been made but much remains to be done.

County Decisions: The Political Process

Recording property deeds, giving free dental exams or innoculations to school children, and synchronizing traffic lights may appear devoid of political overtones, and perhaps so in some counties, but it would be a mistake to think that many such activities are developed in a politics-free environment. Counties exist to supply some needed public services, but not in response to some general public will or always because the state says they must. Counties can adapt state-required services to their constituents' needs, and they can pick and choose among other services states authorize them to provide. Decisions about what and how much, and which regulations to enforce are practical approaches arrived at through political maneuvering, bargaining, and compromise. Everyone who participates in county government plays a proportionate role in the process at some time, including the head of the traffic department and the public health nurse as well as the commissioner, the elected executive, or the largest land developer.

Though partisan party politics may enter in, county politics are really the means to resolve disputes concerning public issues. These conflicts may be based on geography, such as the complaint of central city residents that their county taxes are used to support services in the suburbs, or on ideology such as when the League of Women Voters proposes construction of low- and moderate-income housing in high-income areas, or on self-interest such as the fight of home-owners' associations against high-density development. Even seemingly technical bureaucratic decisions involve politics because technicians have differing views about the best, most efficient way to get things done, and they are constantly pressured to bend the rules and make special exceptions. In short, most decisions are made with regard to people, not administrative rules. There is room for discretion, and rules are always shaped to suit individual or group needs.

Political decisions are reached in various ways: behind closed doors after lengthy discussion and costly concessions have been made by everyone involved; during a public commission meeting; during a staff meeting; and so on. Detailed "inside" descriptions of how final decisions are made prove to be fascinating reading, but they hardly provide a practical orientation. The process is shaped by many factors, including the way formal power is distributed, the informal powers individuals and institutions assume, and traditions. Decision making power in counties generally is decentralized. County commissioners are elected to make overall policy decisions, but the topics they may consider and their courses of action are restricted by the state. Furthermore, their ability to govern is hampered by the existence of several administrative officers—the clerk, the assessor and so on—who are elected to office, and independent or semi-independent boards and commissions, all of whom more or less do as they please. Counties with an elected executive face the power fragmentation problems too, although it may not be as severe as in the traditional commission setup. (See Montgomery County: The Evolution of a Local Government, in Chapter 4.)

County employees—especially the manager and department heads—can exercise considerable discretion despite the fact that they are hired simply to carry out the policies of the commissioners or the executive. Many counties with a professional manager have assigned him a policy making role by authorizing him to evaluate existing programs, recommend new ones and draw up the budget. Even if the authority is not formally delegated, managers and department heads can easily assume powerful roles by default... they are professionals on the job all day every day; most commissioners cannot or do not devote full time to county business.

Decisions of public officials reflect pressures from the general public and from special interests. In this sense, the process operates in two directions: the public or special interest groups can make their wishes known to those in authority, pressing for a decision in their favor. In turn, the politician must at times influence the public, or "pressure" influential groups to support the action he wishes to take.

Counties are also important in partisan party politics. The county has long been the key building block in the

17

American political party system. Both the Democratic and Republican parties are actually confederations of state parties, which, in turn, are confederations of county and city parties. Counties are in a natural position to serve this purpose. American parties are decentralized, yet must cover all the territory within a state, and counties have this kind of geographic base. The importance of the county's political role has fluctuated through the years, but urbanization has made it increasingly powerful. When first set up, county party units were quite important, but as cities grew and assumed political power, central city politicians often dominated the party organization both within the city and the county. Now that the population has shifted to the suburbs, suburban voters in many areas outnumber city voters, and they have made it difficult for city politicians to dominate tne entire county party.

Counties also groom men and women for higher state and national offices. Harry Truman, Spiro Agnew, Kentucky Senator Marlow Cook and former Illinois Governor Richard Ogilvie are examples of men whose political careers began in a county, then led to governor's mansion, seats in state legislatures, offices in the House of Representatives and the Senate, and beyond. County officials, like officeholders in any level of government, are politicians whether they are in the heat of a campaign, in the midst of negotiating a new contract with the sanitation workers, or merely deciding where the new library should be located.

The concept of county government is centuries old. Counties were a part of the initial government of the United States, some of them existed before the nation was formed. Yet, they have been in the background of American government and politics. During the urban explosion, counties began to grow in importance, until now in one vital way or another they affect the lives of nearly all Americans. For these reasons many political scientists feel that the county is at the threshhold of becoming the local government of the future.

18

With this in mind, what are the basics of county government?

Counties are inextricably a part of the total government system. A creation of the states, they derive their power from state authority.

The changes and reforms that are taking place in counties are a response to the developments of an urban society.

County government is the political process of deciding what goods and services should be delivered and which regulations should be enforced, and the administrative process of carrying out these decisions.

Historically counties have been severely limited by state laws. Cities have had the flexibility and autonomy that are part of being independent governments. The development of crippling problems in the cities and the emergence of massive urban counties have forced changes in state attitudes toward more delegation of authority to counties. More flexible, executive oriented governments have resulted.

Though these changes have created vital, dynamic governments, many outmoded features still operate side by side with contemporary ideas. Counties face the future in the midst of changes that have brought new strength, but which have yet to eliminate some crippling state restrictions or the inherent timidity of the counties themselves. Historically counties have been the political grass roots of America; in present day reality they may be developing into *the* local government of the people.

Notes

1. Duncombe, Herbert S., *County Government in America* (Washington, D.C.: National Association of Counties Research Foundation, 1966), p. 23.

2. *Ibid.*, p. 13.

3. National Association of Counties staff, January 1974.

4. *Ibid.* As of December 1973, 50 counties were operating under the council-executive form of government; 36 of these counties are organized by charter and the others are organized in accordance with state law.

5. *From America's Counties Today* (Washington, D.C.: National Association of Counties, 1973), p. 8.

6. *Ibid.*

7. Sofen, Edward, *The Miami Metropolitan Experiment,* 2nd ed. (Garden City, New York: Anchor Books, 1966), p. 13.

8. U.S. Bureau of the Census estimate, October 1973.

9. "Governmental Organization," vol. 1 of *1972 Census of Governments,* (Washington, D.C.: U.S. Bureau of the Census, 1972), p. 10.

10. Advisory Commission on Intergovernmental Relations, *Profile of County Government* (Washington, D.C.: U.S. Government Printing Office, 1972), pp. 5-6.

2. Meeting the Demand for Service

The Scope of County Services

When the modern adventurer sets out in his small boat to sail between continents, he is his own society. The wind supplies the power for transportation; the ocean is his highway. He catches and prepares his own food; he must devise his own methods for disposing of wastes. The sailor is his own doctor, his own judge. He must provide his own sources of recreation. For all practical purposes, he is an independent man.

But as soon as he returns to society, he enters a complex system of dependencies. Even a solitary family living on a farm needs services. There must be electricity for light, gas for heating; they must have roads for transportation. Education, health, hospitals... in the blink of an eye, a whole government complex is necessary if that family is to survive in our society.

A primary purpose of any government is to provide the goods and services citizens cannot provide for themselves. Millions of Americans benefit from services provided by counties, although they may not realize it. Counties fight fires, try to rehabilitate crippled children, operate cemeteries, get rid of garbage and trash, inspect livestock and kill mosquitoes. A handful of them operate zoos and art museums. According to the latest count, counties as a group offer 58 different types of services.[1]

These are not cheap; vast sums are spent on county welfare, courts, education, police protection and other programs. The nation's 3000 counties raised over $11 billion from their citizens in 1970-71, and another $8.5 billion was received from the state and federal governments.[2] Almost their entire income of $20 billion was spent directly on public services. This represents a substantial amount of money, but the figures assume added significance when one realizes that they represent about 20 percent of the revenues and expenditures of all counties, cities, school districts and special districts, or when one charts their increase over a ten-year period.

By any method of calculation, counties are spending a larger share of each taxpayer's income every year, and no reversal of this trend is in sight. What do these dollars buy? Many residents, especially those living in cities or suburban towns, don't know, often because they don't realize how much county programs affect them. They expect the city to pick up their trash, patrol their streets, purify their drinking water and take care of other urban needs. They may assume the county serves only rural areas, operates some courts, and takes care of necessary but uninteresting paper work, such as recording property deeds, marriages, births and deaths. Since these functions do not affect everyday life, many feel no urgency in finding out what the county does until they get their tax bill.

The popular image of counties as local representatives of state government and provider of services for rural areas is partially true and partially false. About 78 percent of the 3000 counties have less than 50,000 residents.[3] One should not assume, however, that these governments operate as they did in the horse and buggy days. Despite appearances the programs of rural counties generally address contemporary needs; many have high priority economic development departments, for example. Though a smaller number of counties have 50,000 or more residents, they serve nearly 150 million people, 74 percent of the 1970 U.S. population![4] The programs of these densely populated counties reflect contemporary, urban concerns... Fairfax County, Virginia has TIP, "turn in a pusher" to stop drug traffic; Sonoma County, California performs abortions and vasectomies for any resident upon request; Montgomery County, Maryland has a commission on the rights of women and another for consumer affairs; and Chatham County and Savannah, Georgia jointly are constructing a $22 million water and sewer system. Some counties are offering services formerly provided by their cities, such as trash pickup, while others specialize in regional functions, such as air and water pollution abatement. The majority of counties offer a mixture of both, with new types of services replacing the old, and important traditional services being updated and expanded. In 1970, 22 Wisconsin counties owned and operated an airport, compared to 15 in 1960. In 1970, 69 Wisconsin counties operated mental health clinics and 44 counties provided day care for retarded children, services virtually nonexistent in 1960.[5] Some counties seem to change almost daily, while others move more slowly. Yet one fact is clear... few counties are stagnating.

One aspect of the popular image of counties—that they are local representatives of state governments—is still true. Counties do spend much time and money doing the tasks states require them to do. However, many states are revising their perspectives toward counties, and as a result, counties are assuming full partnerships with cities in coping with local and regional problems. As urban areas continue to expand, counties can be expected to become a more dominant force in shaping the governmental response to citizens' needs. The following programs of the Nassau County, New York Office of Consumer Affairs demonstrate the all-embracing role a county can play in serving the public.

Nassau County, New York: Programs to Serve Senior Citizens and Youth

The senior citizen program had its inception in February 1971, as a result of discussions at senior citizen clubs about their unique consumer problems.

A recurring complaint centered on fruits and vegetables, which are usually prepackaged by supermarkets in large, family-sized quantities. The elderly, most of whom do not live with large families, were forced to buy more than they needed. Since people on fixed retirement incomes were often hard pressed for the very basics of life, the situation called for action.

The office of consumer affairs solicited the cooperation of every Nassau County supermarket chain to remedy the problem. The stores universally agreed to break up large packages on request or make small quantities available.

This focus on one small problem then brought others to light.

Approximately 170,000 people over the age of 60 live in Nassau. Their consumer problems, while not necessarily unique to their age group, are greatly magnified by their economic and physical limitations.

They are a segment of the population which grows ever poorer. Their buying power shrinks. They live in fear that their life savings, nurtured to cushion their retirement years, will disappear.

Transportation problems make it difficult for them to shop around for better buys, or to return defective merchandise.

They are the particular prey of unscrupulous home improvement operators who foist unnecessary electrical work, roofing, chimney repairs or termite-proofing upon them by means of fear tactics, usually at exorbitant prices, and sometimes with a personal escort to the bank to withdraw money from a savings account. They are also the target of

24

door-to-door salesmen peddling bibles, books and magazines, mail order health cures and insurance.

Through the cooperation of the department of senior citizen affairs, meetings were held with representatives of every senior citizen club in the county. In each club a consumer representative was appointed to take complaints and pass them on to the office of consumer affairs for investigation and resolution.

A special hot line phone number was instituted for the "senior consumer." The phone is manned chiefly by volunteers who are themselves senior citizens. Many have had business experience and are able to offer sympathetic advice or to assist investigators with the complaints. The Consumermobile, a traveling complaint and information unit, visits senior citizens housing projects and community centers.

Speakers from the office of consumer affairs address meetings of senior citizen clubs to discuss consumer problems and offer counsel.

Senior citizen consumers are subject to all the deceptions and abuses that beset the average consumer. What differentiates them from other citizens is their greater need for protection in all areas, whether they are buying apples, aspiran, armchairs or repairing the roof over their heads. The program aims at bringing services to them, and to resolve their complaints with utmost speed and efficiency.

Nassau County wants young people to be smart buyers too, so the office of consumer affairs holds a contest annually to make them aware of potential pitfalls and problems. Students from first grade to twelfth are invited to design posters, pamphlets, games, skits or to use other media for suggesting ways to cope with consumer problems. Several hundred students entered the first contest held in 1972 and the 43 winners had their work exhibited in a "youth-to-youth consumer road show" which traveled from school to school.

The contest and the road show spotlighted consumer

education for both students and teachers, added interest to courses and gave the office of consumer affairs great visibility among the young.

The Services Counties Offer

Virtually all counties—urban or rural—perform eleven basic functions for their constituents, a portion of which, such as assessing property, collecting taxes, and supervising elections, are necessary just to keep the government running. Others bring the state administration closer to home, including the issuing of marriage licenses, fishing licenses, and other permits, and maintaining public records. Counties also spend much time and money keeping the peace and administering justice. Finally, counties offer health and welfare services, and they build and maintain roads and highways.

The Basic Services of County Government

Tax assessment and collection (for counties, in some
   cases cities, school districts and special districts)
Election administration
Judicial administration
Public record keeping
License issuance
Sheriff's office (jails and detention facilities
   as well as police protection)
Agricultural advice
Health
Welfare
Roads and highways
Coroner's office

Counties have been catching thieves, operating jails, overseeing elections, building roads and undertaking the

26

other basic functions since they were established over 300 years ago, and they are required by state constitutions and laws to continue doing so. In this respect, the widely held view of the county as a branch of state government is true. Historically, counties did not choose to undertake these functions because local residents expressed a need for them. They administered the functions because it was convenient for the states. State officials made the overall policies but had to guarantee that they were implemented—uniformly—throughout the jurisdiction. This job was given to counties and they perform it to this day.

Furthermore, most state constitutions and laws specify that persons responsible for these functions be elected to office. Thus, each county has a multitude of elected administrators — sheriff, treasurer, coroner, surveyor, recorder, assessor and so on. This is a holdover from the age of Andrew Jackson when direct democracy was carried to its logical extreme.

County officials and citizens have little influence over the matter — they must commit the tax dollars and they must appoint or elect the personnel to carry out these activities, even though this system diffuses policymaking power and obfuscates lines of responsibility. Functions mandated by the states tie up huge chunks of county budgets. In 1970-71, more than one-fourth of all county direct general expenditures went to support public welfare; about one-sixth went to education, and about one-ninth was spent on both health and highways.[6] Counties are not required to devote so much money to basic services—they are free to decide whether their hospital system should barely meet state standards or be a luxury facility. But the fact remains that even the minimum requirements earmark scanty funds which local officials and citizens might want to spend on other services.

Local officials and the public can try to change the system. They can encourage state legislators to rewrite the laws and initiate an amendment to the constitution, but changes in basic documents are made slowly, though a few counties are making headway. When the Illinois constitution was revised in 1970, giving citizens the opportunity to make the office of coroner appointive instead of elective, voters in eight small counties decided immediately to abolish the elective office in order to stop the drain of tax dollars. Coroners in counties with fewer than 50,000 residents were paid $9000 annually — a figure set by the Illinois legislature. In one small county, the coroner had about seven cases a year, but was given the full salary. Under the new system, appointed coroners can be paid on a per diem basis.[7]

The services which states mandate counties to provide are essential, in most cases, and if given the choice counties probably would continue to offer many of them. But the fact remains that local citizens pay for the services, yet have no direct voice in deciding which are essential and which are not. However, there are ways the public and their elected representatives can adapt required services to local, contemporary needs, and counties are doing just that. Instead of constructing one-lane gravel roads, counties build expressways; instead of counting paper ballots, county election officials use electronic voting machines; and instead of figuring each taxpayer's bill manually, county treasurers use computers. County health programs now include rat control; law enforcement programs include experiments with pretrial release of suspects without bail; and detention programs deal with rehabilitation of teenage offenders. In many ways, traditional services can be and are oriented to the unique requirements of each community.

Urban Services

Several counties, especially the urban ones, offer much more than the basic functions. Their citizens receive many of the services offered by big cities plus some regional ones. Los

Angeles, California; Dade, Florida; Westchester, New York; and others provide elaborate parks, showpiece civic auditoriums, botanical gardens, zoos, comprehensive library systems, and a lot more. Many also take care of the necessities such as sanitation and utilities; they run pollution abatement programs, distribute water, build sewer lines, and collect and dispose of trash and garbage. These urban counties have established themselves as full service governments, responding primarily to constituent needs. Still there are some activities customarily handled locally which counties generally do not undertake. Few counties participate in the urban renewal program even though about 700 counties are classified as "metropolitan" in character; few counties provide housing for indigents, nor do they take charge of mass transit systems. In most places, these functions are still handled by cities or by special districts, which is a reminder that the public served by these counties is essentially suburban. Counties may become more involved in these programs as their suburban populations increase and become more diverse economically and socially.

What accounts for the differences between counties which offer only the basics, and others such as Dade and Los Angeles? At least three factors are involved: the attitude of the state as expressed in its constitution and laws, the aggressiveness of county leadership, and the persistence of citizens. The attitude of the state is crucial; after all, state constitutions and laws established counties and specified what they may and may not do. Today several states still legally regard counties as essentially their field representatives, refusing to allow counties to initiate programs unless approval is granted by the legislature. Washington and Georgia are cases in point. The Washington Supreme Court has described the authority of county governing boards in the state in this way:

Boards of county commissioners have only such powers

as have been granted to them, expressly or by necessary implication, by the constitution and statutes of the state.[8]

This ruling made in 1938 is enforced today, although the state does permit counties to frame and adopt a charter if they wish. In Georgia until November 1972, when a constitutional amendment revised the system, counties wanting to take on new services not specifically authorized were required to propose the project to the legislature, await its approval, and then submit the project to referendum. Fortunately, Georgia counties can now set up many new services by passing an ordinance. In other places, state legislative approval often remains necessary for vital services as well as petty annoyances. In Georgia before the 1972 constitutional revision, it took an act of the legislature to authorize county officials to dispose of abandoned cars. Now that the authority has been granted, one county — Cook — operates a crushing plant to get rid of the nuisance.

State legislatures may grant permission to expand activities quickly and with little fuss if the county officials have a good relationship with their delegation to the legislature, belong to the majority political party, represent interests popular with most legislators, and capitalize on a host of other factors which might or might not relate to citizens' need for the service. But the procedures some county officials have to follow are too often as burdensome as the Georgia counties faced before 1972. Such problems are tragic and frustrating to people who are serious about governing effectively and to a public concerned about who is going to clean up the polluted river from which it obtains drinking water, among other pressing problems.

Yet many states have assumed a much more liberal posture toward counties. At least 19 states allow counties to adopt a charter. This becomes the local "constitution" although its provisions must be consistent with the state constitution and laws, just as state constitutions must conform to the federal one. Counties operating under charter are still obligated to administer some state functions and conform to a variety of state rules, but essentially the parent government takes a hands-off policy. Local officials and the public decide what will be done and how.

Although it is easier to respond to constituent needs when the county has a charter, and some state constitutions do impose severe restrictions, counties adapt to the times and to the peculiarities of their constituents. Allegheny County, Pennsylvania has taken advantage of permission granted by the state legislature to set up a health department. The department inspects restaurants and foods, licenses plumbers, enforces clean air standards in addition to offering more established health services. The county also owns two airports, runs recreation programs and a regional park system, higher education, and economic development services. Allegheny County, in 1973, was the only Pennsylvania county taking part in the Model Cities Program,[9] and is one of the few counties in the nation with a housing coordinator to encourage construction of low- and moderate-income housing. Allegheny County cannot construct subsidized housing, as many cities can, but it can and does encourage distribution of low-income housing throughout its jurisdiction and offers technical assistance to implement its policy.

The fact that there are ways to overcome overbearing state rules is worth repeating. First, the rules rarely limit the level of service — counties are free to provide the bare minimum or the best, most extensive service citizens will pay for. State laws do not prevent the sheriff, for example, from using the most modern techniques of detecting and investigating crimes and apprehending suspects. The Los Angeles County sheriff's department is one of the largest and most esteemed police operations in the nation. Second, county officials can always try to change the rules — they can press the legislature to pass special legislation pertaining exclusively to their county or general legislation allowing all

31

counties to undertake a new service. And third, but perhaps most difficult to achieve, county officials can lobby for a constitutional amendment.

The difficulties encountered by county officials in responding to constituent needs should not be overlooked, but on the other hand, the obstacles to action are not always insurmountable. Officials may use the state's restrictive posture, either deliberately or unconsciously, as a shield from responsibility. When pressured to take actions they find unpalatable politically, county commissioners may protest that the state will not permit it. Citizens unfamiliar with state government may not be able to assess whether the commissioners are offering an excuse or a valid reason. Furthermore, they may not know whom to approach at the state level to seek a change. The legal relationship between the county and the state adds a complicating factor to the politics of providing services.

As long as suburban populations increase, county services will be expanded, county expenses will climb and so will tax bills. The public will come to learn that the county is a full partner with cities and other local governments, and that they can and should take part in deciding what counties will do and who will benefit.

The Financing of Public Services: Charlie's Dilemma

Charlie Williams leaned back in his chair, hand to his forehead, "How am I going to do it!" He leaned forward to look at the figures again, but that didn't change a thing. Wexler County, one of the forty largest in the country, was projecting a $2 million deficit for next year... well, a good finance director could handle that. Charlie could piece together some revenue sharing funds to go with agreements from the commissioners to cut back a little in certain areas.

But $5 million the following year... a $10 million deficit

the year after that. Charlie closed and opened his eyes, took off his glasses for a good wiping, but to no avail. There was no way he could get the county out of this one. Revenue sharing would never amount to more than 3 percent of his revenues. A tax increase? Sure, but the commissioners were worried about the overall tax burden of their citizens, and who wanted to announce a tax increase in an election year? Well, you could always reduce expenditures; after all this was a six-year plan. But where? Wexler was suffering from a crime rise and the sheriff's department was being beefed up. You could never keep salaries down, just from cost of living increases alone. And the new environmental protection program, the consumer affairs commission, the women's rights office, the cable TV program... with everyone in the county so pleased, you couldn't cut back in any of those just when you'd gotten started. Charlie shrugged his shoulders, "What am I going to do?"

Charlie's dilemma is a nationwide problem. Counties everywhere are being squeezed between their rapidly rising costs and revenues which are increasingly difficult to raise. The public demand for services seems nearly insatiable at a time when there is grave resistance to increased taxes. But rising costs have come from the inflation of the paycheck and the prices of goods and services and from an exploding population, as well as the increasing demand for more and better public services. The cost of local government (counties account for about 20 percent) ballooned from $17.0 billion in 1950 to $71.9 billion in 1968, a rate of increase greater than the federal government.[10]

If Charlie is perceptive, he knows he has another problem. In addition to growth and expansion, counties are entering a new phase of change because of a dramatic shift in the composition of the nation's population. The great baby boom following World War II has matured; millions of youngsters have become young adults, just out of college, working and living in the general population. Just ahead of this great bulge is the trough in ages 35 to 45 from the lower birth rate during the depression, and just after it, another trough from the lower birthrate in the late fifties and sixties. At the far end of the scale is the increasing percentage of older persons in our society.

The impact on the demands for public services is tremendous. Just ten years ago counties responsible for schools needed more classrooms and teachers; now they have too many. The changing life style of the great young adult population, with more small families and more unmarrieds living in apartments, has dramatically altered the demand for housing. The elderly require welfare, health and recreational services in unprecedented numbers. The demand for county services not only remains high, but the type and nature of these services are changing as dramatic shifts take place in the make-up of the population.

Within this turbulent context, how do counties handle their finances? Where do they spend their money, and how do they raise it? How do they tax? How are their funds administered, budgeted and controlled?

How Counties Spend Their Money

Every five years the Census Bureau makes a comprehensive survey of county finances, the latest in 1967.[11] According to the graph on page 35, 1967 county spending, which totaled $12.6 billion, was concentrated in four areas:

Public Welfare .... $2.7 billion
Education .... $2.3 billion
Highways .... $2.0 billion
Hospitals .... $1.3 billion

In addition $1.1 billion was spent on financial administration and general control and $3.3 billion on all other expenditures.

The lower half of the graph breaks out "All Other" in

General Expenditure of County Governments, by Function: 1966-67

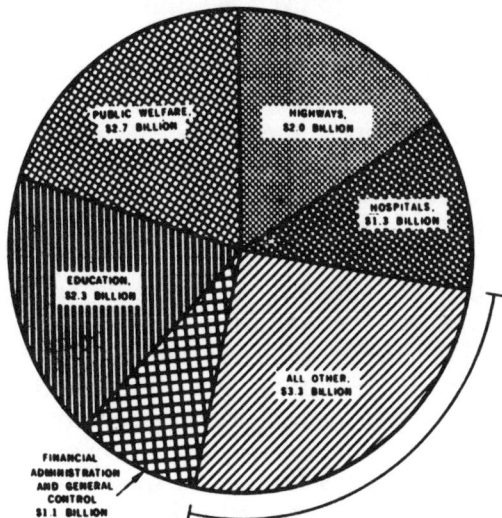

TOTAL, $12.6 BILLION

PUBLIC WELFARE, $2.7 BILLION

HIGHWAYS, $2.0 BILLION

HOSPITALS, $1.3 BILLION

EDUCATION, $2.3 BILLION

ALL OTHER, $3.3 BILLION

FINANCIAL ADMINISTRATION AND GENERAL CONTROL $1.1 BILLION

DETAIL OF "ALL OTHER"

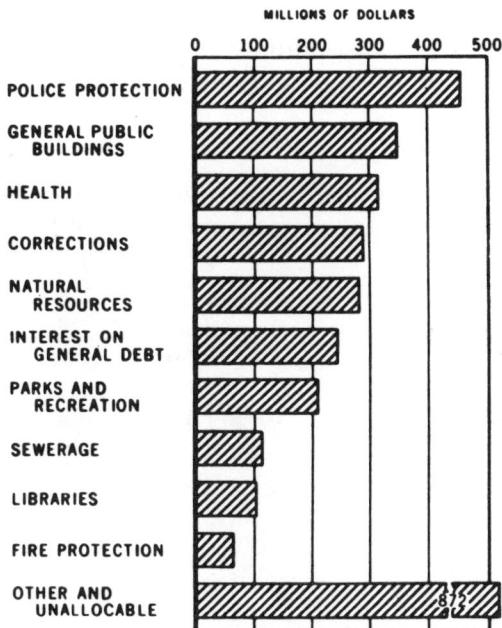

MILLIONS OF DOLLARS

0   100   200   300   400   500

POLICE PROTECTION

GENERAL PUBLIC BUILDINGS

HEALTH

CORRECTIONS

NATURAL RESOURCES

INTEREST ON GENERAL DEBT

PARKS AND RECREATION

SEWERAGE

LIBRARIES

FIRE PROTECTION

OTHER AND UNALLOCABLE

FC/3   U.S. DEPARTMENT OF COMMERCE, BUREAU OF THE CENSUS detail, showing a range of spending, from over $450 million for police protection to over $60 million for fire protection. Counties spend substantial amounts for general public buildings, health, corrections, natural resources, interest on debt, parks and recreation, sewerage, libraries, a host of miscellaneous activities, and the list has grown dramatically in recent years!

How did the picture change in the ten years from 1957? General expenditures more than doubled from $5.9 billion to $12.6 billion. Of the four major categories, highway spending lagged while there were large increases for education, public welfare and especially hospitals. The "All Other" category increased by 138 percent, with large percentage jumps in spending for parks and recreation, libraries, interest and miscellaneous items. Over a third of the expenditures in all categories went for personal services in the form of the county payroll. Current operations account for three-fifths of all county spending, with about one-sixth appropriated for capital outlays.

County Expenditures: 1967 and 1957
(In thousands of dollars)

Item	1967	1957	% Increase
General Expenditures	12,629	5,900	114
Education	2,261	910	149
Highways	1,986	1,240	60
Public Welfare	2,703	1,135	138
Hospitals	1,292	659	196
Financial Administration & General Control	1,115	594	88
All Other	3,273	1,370	139
Police Protection	453	193	135

General Public Buildings	340	174	95
Health	311	132	136
Correction	295	145	103
Natural Resources	281	126	123
Interest	240	90	167
Parks and Recreation	203	67	203
Sewerage	112	103	9
Libraries	103	31	232
Fire Protection	63	26	142
Other and Unallocable	872	273	219

Source: 1967 Census of Governments: County Finance. Bureau of the Census.

Though most counties spend money for the same things, the emphasis varies widely across the nation.[12] In some states, such as Maryland and North Carolina, the counties are responsible for funding the public school system, with education as high as 50 percent or 60 percent of some budgets, compared to the national average of around 18 percent. Colorado, California and Wisconsin require counties to handle public welfare programs, which drives their welfare appropriations much higher than the average. New England counties have modest budgets across the board because the townships in those states handle many activities which counties in other parts of the country undertake. Spending patterns are affected by the state's philosophy toward public spending in general. For example, southern states are more conservative about public welfare than the West and East.

Counties in the South spend the most by far on education, 42.7 percent, while spending the least on public welfare, 5.7 percent. Counties in the West and Northeast make the largest appropriations for public welfare, and the Northeast allocates the highest percentage for the "All Other" category. North Central counties have greater responsibilities for highways and hospitals.

Percentage Expenditures by Regions: 1967

Region	Education	Highway	Public Welfare	Hospital	Finance & Control	All Other
North East	6.4	10.5	28.6	9.3	10.1	35.1
North Central	5.5	25.8	24.8	14.3	9.6	19.0
South	42.7	13.5	5.7	7.4	7.5	22.2
West	7.2	11.8	32.2	10.2	9.0	29.6

Source: 1967 Census of Governments: County Finance. Bureau of the Census.

How Do Counties Raise Funds?

According to the 1967 census of governments there were two primary sources of revenue, property taxes and intergovernmental revenue (grants and shared taxes from states and the federal government). Of $12.8 billion in revenues, $5.3 billion came from property taxes, $5.0 billion from intergovernmental revenues and the remainder from miscellaneous sources—interest, special assessments, and sale of property, among others.

Though revenues from property taxes doubled from 1957 to 1967, other sources grew at a faster rate. Intergovernmental revenues climbed 122 percent from $2.3 billion to $5.0 billion. Other types of taxes and charges increased by over 150 percent, from $869 million to $2.2 billion.

Nationwide there are divergences in the way counties fund themselves. Northeastern counties rely more heavily on property taxes and less on intergovernmental revenues than other areas. In *County Government in America* Herbert Duncombe outlines three patterns of revenue distribution among counties.[13]

Heavy dependence on property taxes — In states such as West Virginia, Montana and North Dakota counties derive 70 percent to 90 percent of all revenues from the property tax with nominal assistance from the states.

Heavy dependence on state sources — Counties in North Carolina, Hawaii and Wisconsin derive 48 to 60 percent of revenues from the states. In these cases, however, substantial revenues, 18 to 40 percent, came from property taxes.

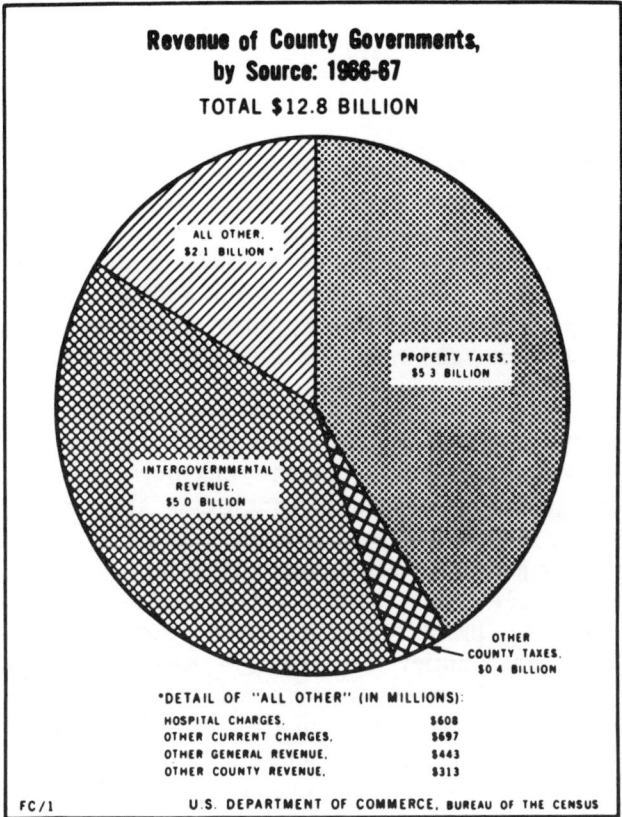

Revenue of County Governments, by Source: 1966-67
TOTAL $12.8 BILLION

ALL OTHER, $2 1 BILLION *

PROPERTY TAXES, $5 3 BILLION

INTERGOVERNMENTAL REVENUE, $5 0 BILLION

OTHER COUNTY TAXES, $0 4 BILLION

*DETAIL OF "ALL OTHER" (IN MILLIONS):

HOSPITAL CHARGES,	$608
OTHER CURRENT CHARGES,	$697
OTHER GENERAL REVENUE,	$443
OTHER COUNTY REVENUE,	$313

FC/1   U.S. DEPARTMENT OF COMMERCE, BUREAU OF THE CENSUS

Dependence on several sources— Counties in Alabama, Kentucky and Washington rely on revenue sources across the board. For example, Kentucky counties earn about 45 percent of their revenues from property taxes, 13 percent from non-property taxes, 14 percent from intergovernmental revenue, 21 percent from current charges and 7 percent from other sources.

County Taxes

Raising money by taxing property has been a tradition in local government since the 19th century. These taxes are levied on three types of property:

Real property such as land, buildings and improvements of a permanent nature. This category is by far the major source of property tax revenues.
Tangible personal property such as household furnishings, machinery, store inventories and automobiles.
Intangible personal property such as stocks, bonds, bank accounts, and other liquid assets.

Property taxes have provided ample revenues for years, and they are not a significant percentage of either property values or personal income. The relative tax burden created by property taxes has stayed constant over the years. They represent a stable source of revenues free from the drastic fluctuations caused by economic changes which are suffered by income taxes.

However, property taxes have been increasingly criticized, and counties have begun to turn to other revenue sources. One problem is the quality of assessment. Assessments are made infrequently, which retards revenue growth and perpetuates inequalities among the classes of property and between high and low valued property. There is a widespread practice of assessing property at some fraction

40

of the full value, which, of course, reduces the tax take. Equally troubling, the percentage of assessed value often varies substantially from county to county within a state. As a result some counties collect more in property taxes which in turn reduces their share of state collected taxes... citizens in these counties pay more total taxes, some of their state payments going to provide services to other counties! In 1957 the New Jersey Supreme Court required a 100 percent valuation basis for property taxes;[14] since then similar decisions have been rendered by the Florida Supreme Court,[15] the Kentucky Court of Appeals;[16] a federal district court in Tennessee[17] and the Chancery Court of Davidson County, Tennessee.[18] It appears that courts in other states will follow these precedents, but today partial valuation is practiced in most areas. There is great political pressure on local assessors to keep property valuations down. The problem is exacerbated by the lack of professional assessment standards in most counties.

Universally the charge of poor administration has been leveled at the property tax system. A primary problem is the financial burden and psychological impact of paying the full amount at one time. This leads to complaints about the intolerable levels of the tax burden, despite the fact that the property tax as a percentage of the gross national product is the same today as in the 1800s.[19] By contrast, income taxes are paid in small installments through deductions from paychecks and sales taxes are collected each time a purchase is made.

Some states set limits to the ways counties can use property tax revenues (37 limit the use of property taxes for general government purposes).[20] These practices tend to retard services and disrupt the budgeting process.

Finally, there has been a serious erosion of the property base because of statutory and constitutional exemptions.

Properties owned by the federal and state governments, educational institutions, religious organizations, and philanthropic and fraternal associations are exempt because theoretically they are used for public purposes. However, carelessness in preparing tax rolls often excludes property owned by these organizations, but not actually used as public facilities. Furthermore, exempting property can cause hardships for counties whose economy relies heavily on education and government services. Often their prime properties go untaxed.

Exceptions are made in many states for property owned by veterans, disadvantaged persons and the elderly, and property used for urban renewal and some business and agricultural purposes. Exemptions are allowed to individuals as a means of making the property tax conform to their ability to pay, however tax experts doubt the wisdom of using property taxes as a means of income distribution, arguing that it is difficult to know where the tax burden lies and what impact changes may have. Industrial properties have traditionally been exempted as a means of attracting new firms; today the practice has ended in all but a few southern and New England states. Redevelopment projects in New York, New Jersey, Missouri and a few other states are tax exempt because it was hoped the tax break would stimulate socially desirable development.

Tangible and intangible personal properties are often exempted because most experts agree that taxation of such properties is ineffective, primarily because they are easy to conceal, assessment is inequitable, administrative costs are high and the taxes impose unequal burdens on taxpayers.

In the face of difficulties with the property tax system and the slower than necessary growth in revenues, counties have turned aggressively to other tax sources. Maryland has adopted a piggyback system by which counties can add up to 50 percent to state income taxes for their own purposes. Other states, such as Michigan, share income taxes with the counties according to population formulas. Some states share sales taxes again according to formula. Many counties can levy sales taxes on selected items, such as gasoline, cigarettes, liquor, and automobile license plates.

Intergovernmental Revenues

States account for the preponderance of outside revenues coming to counties. State assistance takes the form of grants-in-aid and shared taxes. Grants-in-aid are appropriated to counties, without regard to tax intake. They are distributed according to formulas based on population, number of miles of road, school attendance, number on welfare roles, etc. Grants are made for specific purposes or for general purposes without limitation. State-shared taxes are allocated to counties according to fixed formulas. They have the advantage of eliminating the costs of two levels of taxation and of providing the counties with the state enforcement and collection facilities. On the other hand, state collection of taxes deprives the county of the decisions to impose, raise or lower these taxes on its own citizens.

Federal grants are made to counties for an almost infinite array of services, either directly or indirectly through the states (see Chapter 7). Most grants are earmarked for specific projects, but in 1972 the federal government began giving some funds to states, counties and cities to use generally as they wish. Under the general revenue sharing program, the federal government will give these units $30 billion by 1976, with one-third going to the states and the remaining two-thirds to counties and cities. Revenue sharing boosted county budgets by three to five percent during 1972.

Financial Administration and Control

The basic planning and control tool of the counties is the budgeting process. The details of this annual financial plan are specified by state legislation. The process begins with the preparation of next year's estimates by each department. These estimates are then reviewed by the county budget officer, in small counties usually an elected clerk or auditor. Larger counties have budget departments which conduct the review, as well as a review by the elected executive. There may be public hearings during this phase.

The third step is the presentation of budget requests to the governing body. The commissioners review each item in detail, often calling the department heads for consultation. The county budgeting officer may assist. At the end there are usually public hearings to air citizens' views. These hearings offer a comprehensive, well-organized account of a county's forthcoming spending plans and there is no better occasion for the citizen to make his preferences known. The purpose of budgeting is to strike a balance between the needs for expenditures and the amount of funds the county can reasonably expect to receive.

County Debt

If counties relied only on current revenues for funds, the hundreds of millions of dollars in capital expenditures for schools, hospitals, roads and general county buildings would be impossible. As a result counties incur long-term debt, which is amortized by current revenues. There are a variety of state laws restricting the amount of debt, usually in terms of percentages of total assessed value, Michigan at 5 percent, Alabama at 3½ percent as examples.[21] Nationwide limitations range from 2 percent to 20 percent of assumed value. In 1967 counties had outstanding debt of $7.9 billion, of which $1.5 billion was for schools.[22]

Charlie Williams does have a problem, but then Charlie

is the financial manager of a big business. He looks after revenues and expenditures exceeding $100 million for a community of over 300,000 persons. Spending has increased rapidly since 1950, along with the Wexler County population and its demand for public services. Charlie's main concerns are highways, hospitals, education and welfare. His counterparts in other states have varying degrees of concern about the same areas, depending on the state's delegating legislation.

Charlie looks to property taxes and state grants-in-aid and state-shared taxes to pay his bills. In recent years other taxes and intergovernmental revenues have become increasingly important. Charlie manages a substantial debt, limited by state law, to fund capital expenditures for schools, highways and county buildings. He is assisted greatly by the annual budgeting process which details expenditures and revenues so that the two can be kept in balance. During the year expenditures are carefully compared to appropriations to ensure that the budget is followed.

Notes

1. *From America's Counties Today,* (Washington, D.C.: National Association of Counties, 1973), p. 30. Information was based on a representative sample of 1026 counties surveyed by the National Association of Counties, the U.S. Advisory Commission on Intergovernmental Relations and the International City Management Association in 1971.

2. *Ibid.,* p. 5.

3. Advisory Commission on Intergovernmental Relations, *Profile of County Government* (Washington, D.C.: Government Printing Office, 1972), p. 10.

4. *Ibid.*

5. *National Civic Review,* vol. 61, no. 1, January 1972, p. 37.

6. *From America's Counties Today,* p. 5.

7. *National Civic Review,* vol. 61, no. 7, July 1972, p. 363.

8. Condon, George A., "Governing Washington's Counties" (Pullman, Washington: Washington State University and the Washington State Association of County Commissioners, 1968), p. 17.

9. League of Women Voters, Allegheny County Council, "Allegheny County Government" (Pittsburgh, Pennsylvania: League of Women Voters Education Funds of the United States and Pennsylvania, 1971), p. 50.

10. U.S. Bureau of the Census, *1967 Census of Governments,* vol. 4, *Finances of County Governments* (Washington, D.C.: U.S. Government Printing Office, 1967).

11. *Ibid.*

12. *Ibid.*

13. Duncombe, Herbert Sydney, *County Government in America* (Washington, D.C.: National Association of Counties, 1966), p. 112.

14. Smitz v. Township of Middleton, 23 N.J. 580, 130A 2d 15 (1957).

15. Walter v. Schuler, 176 So. 2d 81.

16. Russman v. Lockett, CCH Ky. Tax Rep, pp. 200-766.

17. Louisville and Nashville Railway v. State Board of Equalization, 249 F.Supp. 894 (1966).

18. Southern Railway Co. v. State Board of Equalization, Davidson County Chancery Court, II, Book 77 (1966), p. 191.

19. Johnson, Harry L., ed., *State and Local Tax Problems* (Knoxville, Tennessee: The University of Tennessee Press, 1969), p. 38.

20. *Ibid.*

21. Duncombe, *op. cit.*

22. U.S. Bureau of the Census, *op. cit.*

3.   Government by Regulation

In 1973 construction began on a lookout tower adjacent to the Gettysburg Battlefield. Immediately a contemporary war pitted historic minded citizens and U.S. Park Service officials against the tower developer and some Adams County, Pennsylvania commissioners. The issue of a 307-foot tower, as high as a 30-story building, just 1200 feet from where Lincoln delivered the Address, went to court. The developer maintained that the facility would be "a classroom in the sky, providing a mini-history lesson to prepare tourists for later tours of the battlefield itself." He expected about 750,000 persons a year at $1 each to come for a bird'seye view. A Park Service official countered that the tower would be "a desecration of the historic integrity of the area."

The local board of commissioners was enthusiastic... the tower would boost local pride and the local pocketbook. Tax revenues from a ten percent amusement tax would bring about $56,000 annually, an increase of about $1 for each resident. According to one commissioner, who has a clear view of the tower from his living room, "We're a small county without much to boast about, but this thing is beautiful. It's like someone came in here and built a new Eiffel Tower, right here in Adams County."[1]

Issues as dramatic as the tower or as mundane as the

47

placement of a parking meter often pit citizen against citizen, citizens against business, citizens against county officials and county officials against one another. Ultimately those elected to county office make most of the decisions. The results have far-reaching impact on the lives of their citizens. At some time, with regard to some issue, every citizen is affected directly by the decisions of county officials to regulate — or fail to regulate — the behavior of others. In these political skirmishes some community interests win some of the time, some lose. The astute commissioner or executive will attempt to balance the winners and losers while he is in office — in keeping with the prevailing public sentiment and with an eye toward winning the next election.

All areas of county regulation are important and highly political. Almost all counties have a law enforcement officer — usually the sheriff — to arrest lawbreakers, and many counties, especially urban ones, have rules about protecting the environment, constructing sound buildings, maintaining sanitary restaurants and places of business, drinking too much alcohol, drug abuse and a host of antisocial actions. Theoretically all of these rules protect the entire community, but citizens rarely agree about the greatest dangers. Conservationists, for example, lobby fervently for strict air standards. Just how clean does the manager of the local steel plant feel the air should be?

Today, however, one issue stands out in almost every community... how land will be used. To what extent must open fields be converted to homes, shopping centers and factories and when? It is an all-encompassing issue, touching on population growth, housing, transportation, employment, air pollution, disposal of wastes, water pollution, county finances. Although many think land use is an urban problem, it directly affects rural areas, because urban population and development are growing rapidly outward. In 1960 Prince William County, Virginia was rural. In 1967 it became part of the

Washington, D.C. Standard Metropolitan Statistical Area. In 1950 Santa Clara County, California was agricultural. Though a 300,000 population was not exactly rural, by 1970 the vineyards and fruit farms had given way to manufacturing, and the county was home for over one million people. From 1960 to 1970 the population of Howard County, Maryland soared 71 percent, largely due to the new town of Columbia. Rural areas are becoming increasingly attractive to urbanites anxious to get away to build second homes in the peaceful countryside.

For rural and urban citizens alike, then, what does this rapid development mean? What are the factors contributing to growth? Many are beginning to demand a slowdown in the pace of urbanization. The most vocal — the conservationists, environmentalists, and others — oppose more people and more development because they fear a disruption of the entire ecosystem. Too many people and too much construction can destroy the balance of natural resources, pollute air and water, and force the kind of higher density living which contributes to emotional problems and noise pollution. They argue against the traditional belief that development fattens the public coffers. Rather, argue such sohpisticated groups as the Sierra Club, one must weigh the costs of added public services against the benefits of increased tax revenues from residential, commercial and industrial development.

The environmentalists are relative newcomers to land use politics in urban communities, an area traditionally dominated by business and civic leaders. Decisions about uses of land, such as zoning and subdivisions, usually have been made by governing bodies influenced by the interests of developers, homebuilders, large land owners, and investors in private land development. But the politics of regulating land use is changing. Ordinary citizens are airing their opinions, in many cases to find that the process is more complicated than they thought.

Officials' Power to Regulate Land Use

In a sense, county officials regulate the use of land in almost every decision they make. The approval of a subdivision plat affects the county sewage and water system, the transportation system, employment opportunities, the tax base, county revenues, the quantity and quality of county services, the need for parks, libraries, schools, policemen, firemen, and so on. Most county commissioners have some powers to determine how land will be used though the initiative for developing land rests primarily with private developers, homebuilders, bankers and other businessmen. The county's basic tools, not all equally effective, are the power to formulate comprehensive plans, to zone, to regulate subdivision, to adopt an official map, to enforce building codes, and to build roads, sewers, schools and other community facilities.

Comprehensive Planning

Planning is the formulation of goals and guidelines for the future development of a community. Traditionally county planners have stressed land use, primarily the spatial arrangement of activities in the community, though the process has broadened in recent years to include the economic and social aspects of community development and growth. Planning can be separated into four phases:

establishing community growth and development goals

collecting data about the existing community: its fiscal capabilities, population characteristics, economic structure and other relevant features

projecting these features into the future and preparing

a plan for the community of tomorrow

implementing the plan through zoning and other decisions

The first three phases are handled by professional planners who develop a master or comprehensive plan, essentially a series of maps and policy statements indicating how private land may be used, where schools, parks and other community facilities will be located, and where roads and expressways will be routed. Planners often develop similar guides for particular neighborhoods or districts. These plans may be quite detailed, showing what is proposed for each lot or tract.

Theoretically a citizen could envision the future of his county by analyzing the comprehensive plan, but it is at most a guide for use when county officials make decisions. More important than the plan is the highly political process of developing and implementing it.

Counties generally look upon the planning function as an important one, and the number of counties which plan for future development has been increasing steadily in the past twenty years. A study conducted by the International City Management Association (ICMA) revealed that in 1954 less than half of the counties located in urban areas had official planning agencies. In 1971, a follow-up survey undertaken by the ICMA, the Advisory Commission on Intergovernmental Relations (ACIR) and the National Association of Counties (NACO), revealed that 76 percent of the metropolitan counties and 48 percent of the rural counties which responded were engaged in planning.[2] This is especially impressive when one remembers that planning is usually an optional function; most states do not require counties to plan, but give them the authority to do so. Many counties have been forced into the responsibility by the federal government through its grant-in-aid programs. However, county officials are realizing the need for some comprehensive view of the physical future of their territory. If the federal government had not been involved, they might have taken up planning anyway.

One of the major reasons for comprehensive plans is to deal systematically with all the people who are moving in, to say nothing of the babies being born to those who already live there. During the decade from 1960 to 1970, the U.S. population grew at the rate of 13.3 percent; the average metropolitan area population increased at the rate of 17 percent.[3] About 57 percent of all counties gained population from 1960 to 1970.[4] More than 700 counties now have at least 50,000 citizens and more than 300 of these have at least 100,000 residents.[5] Through long-range planning, county officials can consider the scope of growth problems and the alternatives open to them. The master plan offers a framework for land use decisions such as rezonings, variations in usage, and the issuance of building permits. While land use decisions have always been difficult, today's citizens are forcing their governments to face up to the issues.

Developing the master plan is not a totally rational process; rarely is there agreement about what the future community should be like. It is easy to arrive at consensus over generalities — that planning should be undertaken and that citizens want an orderly, atractive community developed in accordance with the best interests of the entire citizenry. But it is not easy to translate this consensus into a plan affecting specific parcels of land. For example, providing public housing for indigents may be in the best interests of the community, except for those next door to the site. Planning for expressways points the way to convenient travel, unless the new road is routed through one's front yard.

Politics was a dirty word to local planners when they began in the 1920s. To "free planning from politics" the planning agency was usually set up on the periphery of the government. The responsibility was usually assigned to a semi-autonomous commission appointed by the county governing board, the approach still taken in most counties today, though many large urban counties now place the responsibility in a department accountable to the county commission or to the county executive. These counties recognize the reality that, to work in any dynamic way, planning must be brought into the political mainstream of the community.

The planning board or commission usually is composed of the county's leading citizens. In some cases, the head of the county public works department and other relevant departments are ex officio members. Citizens who want to influence what goes on have to become acquainted with the commission members and their special interests. In many counties, planning commissions are dominated by real estate men — developers, homebuilders, owners of large tracts of land. It is natural for county commissioners to appoint them because of their familiarity with land use matters and their commitment to growth and development, a sentiment shared by a majority of citizens in many jurisdictions. In many other counties, however, those opposed to rapid growth and high density development are in control. The appointment of environmentalists, "zero population growth" proponents, and representatives of neighborhood citizens' associations is a fairly recent phenomenon and demonstrates the growing political strength of the antidevelopment advocates.

The commission members do not actually prepare the plan, but they supervise the professional staff which does. The planners, however, gain some independent power simply because they have technical knowledge and training which the commissioners usually lack and because planning is their full-time job, whereas the commissioners are part-time.

If the master plan is to be a framework for decisions about specific pieces of property, then those who influence the content of the plan will influence how the county is developed. In many counties, however, the governing boards do not officially adopt the plans, and it is not clear how much the plans actually influence the day-to-day history of their counties. Nevertheless, equally as many counties follow through on their plans, even though the responsibility for implementation is often in the hands of politicians and bureaucrats who play no role in the formulation.

Scrutiny of master plans today indicates that many are being reoriented, from planning to meet demand, to planning to curb demand. Traditionally, planners tried to anticipate future needs by projecting current population figures and other factors, and then developed plans to meet these needs. Many experts feel that this planning for additional people and industry actually stimulated their development, the plan itself becoming a self-fulfilling prophecy. Communities anticipated more people, made efforts to accommodate them, and, sure enough, the people came. Today, many planners are reflecting the dominant feeling that growth and development are not wanted. They are now setting a limit on the number of people they believe their county can accommodate, then tailoring the projections for housing, transportation, open space and community facilities to take care of that number. Furthermore, planners are suggesting methods for achieving "staged development," that is, making sure that land is left undeveloped until the need for urbanization is essential. Planners in Santa Clara County, California have taken this modified approach.

Santa Clara County, in the San Francisco Bay Area, is now home for over one million, and tripled its population from 1950 to 1970. Two-thirds of the increase was caused by citizens moving to the county. During this same twenty-year period, the economy of the county shifted from agriculture to manufacturing. Huge chunks of farmland were converted into housing. In five short years — from 1962 to 1967 — 7400 acres of farmland were bulldozed and subdivided. In addition much land which once was cultivated now stands vacant. Between 1962 and 1967, 9200 acres of farmland became idle because developments were scattered throughout the county in a leapfrog manner with a little subdivision here, a moderate sized one there. Efficient land use was not the only victim; taxpayers suffered. The county cannot serve the citizens as efficiently as would be possible if all the developments were contiguous.

Mindful of the mistakes of the past, the Santa Clara County Planning Commission is urging that the remaining land be utilized for its "most appropriate uses." Planners believe the county has ample resources to accommodate foreseeable population increases, although they have not ruled out the need for a growth policy. They believe that staged development, if adhered to strictly, can lead to an orderly, desirable level of urbanization. Thus they are trying to stall development in some sections by zoning property for open space, conservation and agriculture. Through the years, as contiguous developed areas expand to meet the open spaces, the large lots can be rezoned for higher densities and urban uses.[6]

There are several limitations to planning as a land use tool. As mentioned earlier, in the great percentage of counties where planning is undertaken by a semi-independent commission, the activity is not within the mainstream of policy setting and administration. County commissioners make the zoning decisions; the planning commissioner does not, although he and his staff may give advice, and often this advice is carefully considered. No matter who draws up the plans, however, the county governing authorities are not obligated to adopt it as their official policy. At least 900 counties had adopted a plan by 1971, according to the Advisory Commission on Intergovernmental Relations,[7] but in the view of some critics of planning, "more communities appear to be 'doing' planning than doing anything about it."[8]

Some would argue that even if the plan were adopted and attempts were made to implement it, the objectives would not be realized because other departments and agencies responsible for planning and operating specialized functional programs — like the highway department — proceed with little regard for the comprehensive plan.[9] Many highway departments, for instance, are not required to coordinate their five-

55

year plans with the county general plan, and no one in a position of overall authority in the county forces them to do so. Specialized agencies and departments have the edge over general planners when it comes to implementing plans. First, the specialists are guided by accepted standards and can quantify the need for more services. Highway planners, for example, can count traffic flows, conduct origin and destination studies and build models. Such concrete standards are not available to comprehensive planners.

Second, departments both plan and implement; they decide where roads should be, for example, and then build them or hire private companies to do so. Comprehensive planners do not have implementation powers; their only hope is to persuade the county commissioners and departments to abide by the plan.

Third, specialized agencies often are supported by several clients and constituents who add their political backing. Highway agencies, once again, are supported by cement firms, auto manufacturers, rubber, oil and trucking interests. Comprehensive planners have advocates too, but they are usually less powerful and less focused in their intent than the clients of specialized departments.

Besides, no one can completely and accurately chart future development and economic conditions. When will landowners make their land available for development? When will it be developed? What pressures will the marketplace bring to bear on particular parcels of land? Because of the tremendous number of unpredictable and interrelated factors, county officials must keep their options open. Even in counties with the most sophisticated planning, zoning decisions remain political. It has been said that rezoning, especially requests for changes from single-family residential to higher-density residential or commercial, are the most hotly contested issues, the crux of land-use politics in the suburbs, where land-use politics are commonly the most overriding concern. In *Politics of Land Use* by Linowes and

56

Allensworth, the situation was described aptly: "It was never intended that zoning be used for the people in general. It was and is known that zoning will work for the interests of those who have the power over it..."[10]

Zoning as a Control of Land Use

It is through zoning decisions that county officials substantially contribute to the implementation of the comprehensive plan — or to its undoing. The entire county is divided into zones or districts which specify the types of development permitted. Three kinds of zones are generally provided for— commercial, residential and industrial — but the county may provide for subzones within each category, thus further refining the type of development allowed. For example, a residential zone may be designated for single-family detached homes, townhouses, garden apartments, high-rise apartments and so on. Zoning regulations usually include other restrictions such as stipulating the maximum height of buildings, the proportion of a lot a structure may cover, the setback and side lines, and in the case of multifamily and business uses, the amount of off-street parking to be provided. The purpose of zoning is to separate incompatible uses of land, the factories from the luxury homes, etc. However, in recent years a few cities and counties have broken away from the rigid tradition and have allowed a mixture of commercial and residential uses within the same zones. Many local governments have also permitted mixtures of densities and more flexible layouts for residential areas. Some, for example, have given the subdivider the option of substituting for the traditional block of homes with individual yards, a clustered development where homes are built on small lots in close proximity while the remaining land is left as open space.

Zoning policy is given the force of law when the county

legislature adopts a zoning ordinance. The ordinance usually consists of a text describing the various zones and uses permitted in them, and a map showing the legally stipulated use for each parcel of land. The ordinance is enforced when county officials issue — or refuse to issue — building permits.

Zoning traditionally is a function of municipalities. However in recent years, especially since 1968, counties have become involved. According to a 1971 survey conducted by the Advisory Committee on Intergovernmental Relations, the National Association of Counties, and the International City Management Association, at least 500 counties have authority to zone.[11] While the number may seem small in comparison to the total number of counties, most of the counties which zone are located in metropolitan areas where the most people and the greatest need for regulation exist. Also, only in recent years have counties been given authority to zone. As late as 1966, twelve states withheld this power from counties.[12] States even have been restrictive in granting zoning powers to cities, by refusing to acknowledge that the authority was part of a city's home rule powers.

In theory zoning seems straightforward enough: the county governing board, with staff assistance, determines the boundaries of the various zones and then adopts an ordinance and a zoning map specifying the uses allowed in each one. It doesn't work that way. County officials have authority to change their minds. They reserve the option to amend the text of the zoning ordinance and its accompanying map, and to permit special exceptions and variations within zones.

County commissioners have final authority in rezoning cases. Unlike planning, where many decisions are made by professionals and commissioners of semi-independent agencies, zoning decisions are made by those elected to govern. In many counties, the planning agency advises the governing board, and their advice may be tantamount to a final decision in routine cases, but in anything important, the governing body jealously guards its authority. Even in counties with an

58

elected executive, zoning is considered a legislative function.

Most counties which zone have set up a semi-autonomous board of appeals, board of adjustments, and so on, to hear requests for special use permits or variances — that is, permission to establish a use not typical in a particular zoning category but permitted under certain conditions (such as location of a hairdresser in a residential area), or permission to establish a use not allowed under the zoning ordinance but permitted if compliance with the ordinance would involve "unnecessary hardship" or "practical difficulty." While some of these requests may be hotly contested, most cases heard by zoning boards are routine.

Once the zoning ordinance and map are adopted, county commissioners usually do not take the initiative in using zoning to guide development. Instead, the first step is taken by landowners or developers who usually seek permission from the governing board to develop the land at a higher density or more intense use than prescribed on the zoning map. Landowners usually take this action in response to market pressures or to increase the value of their property. Most rezoning requests are for undeveloped land zoned single-family residential, although rezonings are also sought for improved land. Developers usually argue on economic grounds: more intense uses are necessary to accommodate more people and to attract more businesses, which means more revenue for the county and an increase in the value of property, which leads to a higher tax assessment and, again, more income for the county.

Not everyone in the county may agree. As mentioned earlier, an antidevelopment attitude is now prevalent in most urban counties, but those opposed to rezoning which permits higher densities must monitor the zoning process carefully to know when and to whom they should present their case. In many counties this means they must find out when and where rezoning applications are filed, study the applications, find out when the public hearing is scheduled, and prepare solid testimony to present at the hearing. Counties rarely send public notices to residents of neighborhoods who might be affected by rezoning — it is up to residents to ferret out the information for themselves.

Rezonings are typically opposed by residents and owners of single family homes who group themselves into citizens' associations or neighborhood improvement associations. In recent years these organizations have been joined by environmentalists, conservationists, those promoting zero population growth, and others. Many citizens' associations are quite familiar with rezoning procedures and the public officials who make the decisions; others are not. Some appear at public rezoning hearings to present sound arguments for not granting the zoning change in many cases prepared by consultants, professional planners or zoning lawyers; others are less skillful.

Both developers seeking rezonings and citizens' associations who oppose them base their positions on economics. Citizens strive to maintain low-density residential zones in order "to keep taxes low." They maintain that single-family homes on large lots are less expensive for the county to serve than are high-density apartment complexes. Actually, the "hidden agenda" of many citizens' associations is to prevent construction of housing—either apartments or single-family houses—for persons with low or moderate incomes. On the other hand, environmentalists typically base their opposition on grounds that natural resources will be destroyed, air and water pollution will increase, sewage systems will be overloaded, and traffic congestion will increase the frustrations of commuters and shoppers.

The county officials have to decide whose values will be served. In many ways, development interests have the edge over citizens. Landowners and homebuilders have money, and they spend it on skillful, experienced consultants and zoning lawyers. Furthermore, they have been involved in zoning decisions for years. Representatives of citizens' interests are relative newcomers to zoning politics, having become a force to contend with only within the last ten to fifteen years, and they have no money. Most groups cannot afford expensive technical and legal advice. But they have strength in numbers and the greater the following, the more likely it is that county officials will pay attention. This is one of the reasons that neighborhood citizens' associations combine into citywide federations. Then a member association can claim to represent far more people than it actually does.

Democratic ideology and contemporary values of good and bad are tremendous assets for citizens' groups. If a citizens' association can claim to speak for thousands of constituents — against a single, profit-minded developer — then it must represent the majority interest. In the glare of publicity, what good politician would ignore the will of the people and side with a special interest? Citizens, especially environmentalists, couch their anti-rezoning arguments in terms of preserving natural resources. Higher densities lead to many evils, and an elected official cannot appear to decide in favor of air pollution, more crowding, traffic jams and loss of open space.

Contending parties have at least two legitimate avenues to county commissioners. They may lobby and appear at public hearings or they may try to influence the selection of candidates for the next election. Real estate interests and citizens' associations tend to be nonpartisan in local politics. Their concern is more about the candidate's posture toward land use than the party label; however in some sections of the country one party more consistently supports the same policies as they do. In partisan communities in the North, citizens' groups seem to find more in common with the Republican party, while in the southern and border states the Democratic party is more frequently the ally. In all parts of the nation citizens' groups are more apt to work with liberals than conservatives of either party.[13]

The job of influencing candidate selection has become

easier for citizens' groups as the environmental and population control movements have gained momentum. In many counties, candidates are running on antidevelopment platforms. Dade County, Florida is a good example. The 1972 election saw four candidates band together as the Committee for Sane Growth. All four were elected to the county governing board, one as the mayor or presiding officer. Their platform called for a halt to rezoning if conditions for maintaining a healthy environment could not be met.[14] This situation has arisen in other counties as well.

County commissioners can do more than sit back and wait for the filing of rezoning applications. They can initiate rezonings, declare moratoriums on rezonings, and can set up new categories for open space or agricultural uses.

Montgomery County, Maryland, bordering Washington, D.C., is "downzoning" some residential and commercial areas. The county council amended the text of the zoning ordinance to decrease allowable densities in an effort to prevent development of open space and to cut down on commercial area congestion. In the predominantly rural "up county" as much as 200,000 acres will come under the five-acre zone, which increases the minimum lot for development from one and one-half to two acres, to five, with obvious results.

Dade County, Florida, under the leadership of the antidevelopment commissioners, is using the rezoning moratorium approach. County commissioners will not consider rezoning requests for particular sections of the county. The halt was approved by voters in a referendum.[15] County officials in three California jurisdictions—Marin, Santa Cruz and Monterey—set up new zoning categories for open space and agriculture.[16] In 1965 Marin County placed two-thirds of its 300,000 acres into an agricultural preserve. Since 1965, 100,000 of these acres have been put under contract. Under this arrangement local governments in the county may reduce property tax assessments if landowners agree to retain their land for farm purposes for a fixed period of years. Then in

1971 the land in the agricultural zone was "downzoned" from one dwelling per three acres to larger parcels; by 1972, 60,000 acres of Marin County agricultural land had been zoned for 60-acre minimum lots. Santa Cruz and Monterey counties — both endowed with rich farmland — have already zoned substantial portions of land for large lots only. In Santa Cruz County, about half the county will be zoned for 20-acre or larger lots; in Monterey County about one-third of the county will be reserved for 40-acre lots.

Unfortunately, attempts to downzone and preserve open space raise some ugly social issues. Zoning policy is also housing policy in a very real sense. If substantial portions of the county are zoned for single-family houses on large lots, luxury homes will be built. While in many counties there may be a legitimate demand for expensive homes, there is probably a greater need for houses and apartments which people with low and moderate incomes can afford. The need will probably become greater as industry — and jobs — move from central cities to suburban counties. Through zoning decisions county officials have the power to exclude the less affluent — who are usually black or elderly — and contribute to residential segregation, or to offer more opportunities for social mobility to these people. However, the case against large-lot and open-space zoning is not clear-cut, because these techniques do influence the location, timing and scale of development, enabling officials to better prepare for the influx of people and their demands for public services.

Limitations to Zoning Powers

Zoning is one of the county's most powerful land use tools, but the ability of county officials to influence county-wide development often stops at the city line. Most counties cannot zone within a municipality. Furthermore, many states grant cities authority to zone for contiguous unincorporated areas beyond the city limit—say three to five miles. Although in a few states, the reverse situation is true—urban counties are authorized to review municipal zoning and subdivision decisions—this is not typical. Thus county zoning policies can be relatively insignificant if most of the jurisdiction is incorporated. If rules about annexing and incorporating are lenient, county officials and citizens may find zoning decisions reversed when the territory becomes part of a city. In fact, county zoning could encourage defensive incorporations. Black Jack, Missouri is a case in point.

Prior to 1970 Black Jack was an unincorporated section of St. Louis County. County officials viewed the 2.7 square mile undeveloped area as a suitable location for a multifamily, moderate-income housing complex, and began negotiations with the U.S. Department of Housing and Urban Development for financial assistance. The complex would be within a short commute of two major industrial facilities—McDonnell-Douglas Aircraft and Ford Motor Company.

Residents of the Black Jack community opposed the county's action and were successful in reversing it by becoming a municipal corporation. Within a few weeks of incorporation, the new city adopted a zoning ordinance that does not permit multifamily residential uses. T he Black Jack Improvement Association, in the vanguard of the incorporation drive, circulated a newsletter citing objections to the housing project: lack of employment opportunities nearby, lack of transportation, devaluation of neighboring property, projected school tax deficits, and crowding of low-income families into a close space causing the potential for disturbances that require more police.

Once Black Jack became a municipality, county officials lost all jurisdiction over zoning within its borders. However, the city zoning ordinance is being challenged by the American Civil Liberties Union and the U.S. Department of Justice on grounds that it is racially discriminatory.[17]

Although a weakness of county zoning power is the restricted territory covered by it, recent trends indicate that county responsibilities may increase. If county zoning authority is enhanced it will be an unintended consequence of actions taken by state governments to curb the creation of more municipalities and special districts, not necessarily because state officials wanted to give counties more land use control.

Other Ways to Regulate Land Use

There are indirect methods of influencing land use, such as deciding where sewer and water lines should go and whether homes, commercial and industrial establishments will be granted permission to hook up to them. Without sewer and water lines — or the high probability they will be built — builders will not waste their time trying to achieve rezonings and then constructing homes and shopping centers.

Montgomery County, Maryland is a good example. Montgomery, five other counties and Washington, D.C. all rely on a single waste treatment plant to treat millions of gallons of raw sewage daily. Montgomery County alone contributes about 67 million gallons each day. In 1970, it became apparent that the plant could not keep up with the increases in sewage brought on by increases in population, and the governments in the area agreed to do something about it. In a memorandum of understanding, the jurisdictions agreed, essentially, to a moratorium on future sewer hookups. To Montgomery County, this meant that no additional permits for sewer connections were to be granted until another waste treatment plant could be constructed. This decision was made to cope with a crisis situation, to relieve further pollution of two rivers running through the Washington, D.C. area. But the short-run consequences, in Montgomery County at least, had the opposite effect, and the long-run consequences may not be beneficial either.

At the time the sewer ban became effective, many builders had been given permission to build and to hook up to sewer lines. Instead of staging this development over several years as they had planned initially, the builders began building with a flurry, fearful that the county would revoke permits already granted. Thus more homes, shopping centers, and other facilities were constructed than had been anticipated during this time, leading to more people and more sewage. In the meantime, some of the long-range consequences of the sewer moratorium are already being felt. Anticipating an even more severe housing shortage than now exists, prices of homes have skyrocketed. The county has few homes in the price range low- to moderate-income families can afford, and no homes in this price range are being constructed. The longer the moratorium remains in effect, the more serious the housing shortage will become. Eventually, construction in the county could come to a halt, with unprecedented effects on the tax base and the prices of homes. Environmentalists and forces opposing development may believe they have won a victory, but it is probable that the political pressures against the "no growth" policy will force some concessions.

Other Regulatory Functions

The authority of counties to regulate for the public good extends to activities other than developing and using land. Counties also enforce clean air and water standards, restrict the activities of lawbreakers, make sure public places — restaurants, motels and the like — are sanitary, and that buildings are safe enough for working and living.

Surely law enforcement is the most visible aspect of county regulation. Every county has a sheriff or a police chief responsible for maintaining law and order. Law enforcement personnel patrol highways and neighborhoods, use radar to catch speeders, operate radio networks, investigate crimes, make arrests, and maintain jails. Sheriffs are also officers of the court and as such they serve warrants and subpoenas and collect delinquent taxes.

County health officers are also becoming more involved in regulatory activities. They inspect hotels, food stores, and dairy farms plus public facilities such as water supplies, sewage disposal plants and swimming pools to insure compliance with sanitation standards. As alarm over environmental pollution has increased, health officers have begun enforcing county air and water pollution standards. It was the director of the Jefferson County, Alabama Health Department who was instrumental in closing 23 steel firms to avert a major air pollution crisis in the Birmingham area in 1971.[18]

Most counties have the authority to establish and enforce building codes. The basic purpose of these codes is to insure that buildings are structurally sound, relatively free of fire hazards, and sanitary. H. Bemis Lawrence, former commissioner of Jefferson County, Kentucky described the elements of a comprehensive code enforcement program:

If such a program is to be of value to both the governing and the governed, it is necessary that a comprehensive system of codes be adopted. The term comprehensive means the embracing of all ordinances of a locality regulating minimum conditions of use, construction, alteration, repair, maintenance, and demolition of private property within the entire community. As a general rule, most ordinances are contained in the building, plumbing, electrical, fire prevention, housing and zoning and subdivision regulations. However, a comprehensive system of codes would include other miscellaneous enactments dealing with such specific hazards as sanitation, gas boiler installations, and steam fitting, air pollution, and heating and ventilating. The codes should be correlated and be so worded, numbered, indexed, and composed, that any citizen will be able to find out what the requirements are.[19]

The program undertaken by Nassau County, New York shows how one county is regulating home construction.

Nassau County Protects Homeowners

To safeguard homeowners from the abuses of itinerant contractors, repairmen and remodelers, an ordinance was passed requiring that all persons operating home improvement businesses in Nassau County be licensed. The office of consumer affairs began issuing these licenses on January 1, 1972. Home improvement complaints had constituted the largest single problem area for the office of consumer affairs during its three years in operation, with dissatisfaction increasing each year at a greater rate than in all other categories. Nassau is predominantly a county of homeowners. Thus firms providing maintenance, repair and remodeling service form a sizable industry. The complaints indicated that Nassau consumers were being bilked out of millions of dollars because of shoddy workmanship, unfinished jobs or unfulfilled contracts.

Applications were issued to more than 4000 persons engaged in home improvement businesses, ranging from one-man operations to giant home corporations. Firms headquartered elsewhere but working in the county were also required to be licensed. Because a major goal of the program was to rid the county of unethical itinerants, applications called for a permanent place of business, photos of company officers, fingerprints and resumés of experience. Applicants were investigated, and previous complaints were reviewed.

Many types of home improvement businesses were covered: general contractors, aluminum siding contractors, carpenters, burglar- and fire-alarm dealers, fence installers, air-conditioning contractors, landscape contractors and others.

The law empowers the commissioner of consumer affairs to refuse, suspend or revoke a license if, after a hearing, the contractor is shown to have failed continually to perform his contracts, employed untrustworthy management personnel, engaged in fraud or misrepresentation, or made false statements in his application for a license. Violations are also punishable by fines of up to $500 or imprisonment for not more than 60 days, or both. The annual fee for the license is $50. During 1971 approximately 2000 home improvement complaints were received and investigated, and approximately $25,000 was returned to consumers in refunds and adjustments. Violation notices were issued to, and fines paid by, 182 persons. Five licenses were suspended and one license was revoked. It is anticipated that the licensing program, with its threat of revocation, will serve to eliminate many of the problems that have caused consumers to complain.

The politics of regulation is perhaps the most intense and fascinating form of politics in urban counties. While the county's authority to regulate for the public good may appear simple enough in theory, practical politics and daily decision-making leave little time for philosophical concepts. Deciding who constitutes the public, let alone what is good for it, is a tedious balancing act for county officials.

Notes

1. *The Washington Post,* Sunday, October 28, 1973, p. A1.
2. *From America's Counties Today* (Washington, D.C.: National Association of Counties, 1973), p. 33.
3. U.S. Bureau of the Census staff, October 1973.
4. *From America's Counties Today,* p. 3.
5. Advisory Commission on Intergovernmental Relations, *Profile of County Government* (Washington, D.C.:

U.S. Government Printing Office, 1972), p. 10.

6. "A Policy Plan for the Baylands of Santa Clara County," (San Jose, California: Santa Clara County, California Planning Department, October 1972), p. 9.

7. Advisory Commission on Intergovernmental Relations, *op. cit.*, p. 32.

8. Linowes, R. Robert and Don T. Allensworth, *The Politics of Land Use,* (New York: Praeger Publishers, 1973), p. 32.

9. *Ibid.,* p. 39.

10. *Ibid.,* p. 65.

11. Advisory Commission on Intergovernmental Relations, *op. cit.,* p. 32.

12. *Ibid.*

13. Linowes and Allensworth, *op. cit.,* p. 138.

14. Reilly, William K., ed., *The Use of Land: A Citizens' Policy Guide to Urban Growth,* (New York: Thomas Y. Crowell Company, 1973), p. 38.

15. *Ibid.,* p. 137.

16. *Ibid.,* p. 120-121.

17. *Ibid.,* p. 89-91.

18. Rosenbaum, Walter A., *The Politics of Environmental Concern,* (New York: Praeger Publishers, 1973), p. 4.

19. Lawrence, H. Bemis, "Code Administration and Enforcement," in *Guide to County Organization and Management,* (Washington, D.C.: National Association of Counties, 1968), p. 377.

4. The Politics of Public Decisions

> . . . it is not the law's concern that any one class in a state should live surpassingly well. Rather it contrives good life for the whole state, harmonizing the citizens by persuasion and compulsion, and making them share with one another the advantage which each class can contribute to the community. It is the law which produces such men in the city; not in order to leave each man free to turn where he will, but that it may itself use them to bind the city together.
>
> *The Republic,* Book VII

Land use decisions are a fair example of how most issues are handled by county governments. The homeowners' associations, developers, planning commissions, and councils of Chapter 3 could instead be other local entities involved in other issues, but the process of political bargaining, compromise and sometimes intense conflict would remain essentially the same. Whether major or mundane, public issues reflect — and generate — differences of opinion within the community and its government. Widening a road, installing lights at a tennis court, teaching sex education, or closing a street may not seem earth shattering events, but they can and do set off heated controversies.

Public officials resolve these conflicts through their final decisions. In the end they separate the winners from the losers. Once the decision is made, they must implement it, either directly or by delegation to county employees. On top of that they are responsible for carrying out programs set up by officials who held office before they did. County decision-making may appear simpler than it is; the process is complicated by the way the formal governing powers themselves are distributed. Collectively, both elected and appointed county officials have immense power to manage conflicts and make decisions, but individually each has only a fraction of that power. Of course some have been granted more authority than others, for example, a county commissioner as opposed to the public health nurse; and formal powers are often augmented by informal ones, such as force of personality, leadership ability, tenure in office, etc. Nevertheless, one cannot understand county governance without some knowledge of how power is distributed among the agencies and offices of the government, or how it is affected by the array of citizens and special interest groups of the community. The electoral system, the procedures for nominating and electing public officeholders, also bears on the authority those persons exercise once in office.

Who Has the Authority?

In 87 percent of all counties, overall authority is vested in a county commission. The commission is usually referred to as the governing body, but it is not the only agency with the power or responsibility to govern.

The commission in a majority of counties consists of from three to five members. Some counties have larger boards and some smaller, as mentioned in Chapter 1. Collectively these commissioners have two responsibilities: to pass local laws, and to administer county programs. In a few southern states, commissioners perform a limited number of judicial functions as well. The principle of combining legislative and executive functions is traceable directly to the British heritage. Originally, American cities were also governed by commissions which exercised lawmaking and executive powers. Beginning in the 1820s, however, cities began to separate the two, electing a mayor to be the top executive and retaining the council or commission to make laws. Apparently they adopted this new structure to emulate the highly regarded federal system, rather than as a response to any practical considerations of politics and administration.[1] Today most big cities continue to divide governing responsibilities between the mayor and the council.

The separation of powers principle bypassed counties, or what may prove to be the case, caught up with them about 175 to 200 years later. Today only 50 counties have an elected executive, the county equivalent of a mayor; however, these 50 counties govern close to 27 million people. About ten of these are consolidated city-county governments, such as San Francisco and Denver, which are customarily regarded as cities. Of the remaining 40, all except three shifted to this new form of government within the last 20 years. In fact, 30 of the 40 counties elected their first executive in the 1960s and 1970s, and ten of these created the position since 1970.[2] As states allow counties to assume more functions, and as urbanization increases, the trend toward the executive system may accelerate.

At first glance, it would appear that the county commission has tremendous power. They decide how the county funds will be spent; they pass resolutions, ordinances and regulations; they hire and fire personnel and supervise the administration of county programs. They carry out additional functions assigned by the state. However, several factors limit their prerogatives.

One is salary. Despite the fact that county government could easily consume every waking hour, commissioners can rarely afford to devote much time to county affairs because

73

the pay is so low. A commissioner elected at large in a typical metropolitan county receives only $10,000 a year; his colleague in a rural county receives roughly $4000. Commissioners elected from districts are usually paid even less — $7500 annually in a typical metropolitan county and only $3000 in a rural one. Obviously, most commissioners must have full-time jobs, and must manage the county's business during their spare time.

Median At-Large Members of County Governing Bodies, Length of Term and Annual Salary

Classification	No. of counties reporting	Members	Median range length of term (in years)	Salary
Total, all counties	380	3	2-4	$ 5,250
Metropolitan status				
Metro	80	3	2-4	10,000
Nonmetro	300	3	2-4	4,200
Professional management				
With administrator	65	3	2-4	3,400
Without administrator	305	3	2-4	5,460

Median Single-Member District Members of County Governing Bodies, Length of Term, Annual Salary

Classification	No. of counties reporting	Members	Median range length of term (in years)	Salary
Total, all counties	519	4	2-4	$3,500
Metropolitan status				
Metro	60	5	4	7,500
Nonmetro	590	4	2-4	3,200
Professional management				
With administrator	116	5	4	4,500
Without administrator	403	4	2-4	3,400

74

Source: Urban Data Service, Jean Gansel and George Howe *County Government Organization and Services,* (Washington, D.C.: International City Management Association, vol. 3, no. 5, May 1971), p. 3.

Most commissions are basically leaderless groups of officials, which fact often detracts from the authority of the body, though it may enhance the power of an individual member. Every commission is led, in a pro forma fashion at least, by a presiding officer. In some counties, the commission president, presiding judge, or whatever the title may be, is elected to this post by the voters, but in as many other counties, the officer is selected by the fellow commissioners. In some cases, additional responsibilities come with the office. In Texas, for example, the county judge, elected at large to preside over the commissioners' court, is responsible for preparing the budget, serving on the county election board with the sheriff and the county clerk, acting as ex-officio school superintendent and as a member of the juvenile board. Furthermore, the presiding officer is the judge of the county court, a judicial post. However, the judge has only one vote on the commission and no veto power.[3] Any executive or leadership role he assumes is a tribute to his personality, if not indefatigability, political savvy, tenure, and so on.

Under the commission system, the public may have a hard time finding out who is in charge. If developers are planning a high-rise, luxury condominium on the shoreline, to whom should the conservationists appeal? If the emergency room of the county hospital is understaffed, to whom should neglected patients air their complaints? If subdivisions are built without regard for adequate sewage treatment facilities, to whom should the aggrieved parties go to force remedial action? When the county is governed by a commission of three to five with equal authority, all of them can manage, rather easily at times and on specific issues, to avoid being put on the spot. Commissioners in some counties simply refuse to make decisions. They deliberate for hours over relatively inconsequential issues and the necessity of spending small sums of money.

However, the astute politician always makes sure his constituents know what he does for them, just as he keeps a low profile on issues they wouldn't be so happy about. As one supervisor of a large county put it, "The great technique of staying in office is to take credit for all the good things and blame somebody else for all the bad."[4] If a new boulevard is being dedicated in his district the supervisor is on the scene, but if someone calls his office to complain, the constituent is likely to be referred to someone else. The commission system gives him opportunities to grant favors and to undertake projects with little interference from his colleagues. To a great extent, under this system constituents get a great deal of what they want, especially if the commissioners are elected from districts.

How so? By a tradition as old as government itself — logrolling. Each commissioner looks first to his constituents' needs. When he asks for money to build a small playground, his colleagues grant it willingly, knowing that when they want a new youth center or library their backs will be scratched. Two reporters described how this system works in Los Angeles County, California.

"Shortly after 9 a.m., the chairman of the board calls the meeting to order and begins what must be the fastest legislative process in the history of the free world. Working from the printed agenda (the board chairman) calls out the items under consideration by number and in groups.

"Items one through five," he says.

"I'll move," says (one supervisor).

"Second," says (another).

"So ordered," says (the chairman).

You try to study the printed description of the items just approved and realize that the board is adopting them literally faster than you can read them.

"Items 29 through 52," says (the chairman), adding the department requesting them, "county engineer." You glance at the agenda: one item is for $203,000; another for $806,000; another for $906,000.

"I'll move," says (one supervisor).

"Second," says (another).

"So ordered."

"At one week's meeting of the board, one of us arrived 30 minutes late, too late that day to hear the action of any of 126 regular agenda items: each had already been adopted.

"At one recent three-hour board meeting, there was absolutely no challenge or argument among the supervisors or between the supervisors and any of their staff... At one point, after 120 items involving millions of dollars had been acted on, (one supervisor) observed happily: 'There hasn't been a single objection to any motion.'"

The reporters continued:

"One of the most remarkable phenomena in (Los Angeles) county government is its building program. (The supervisors) insist that new capital projects are required by the state and by the sharp increase in the demand for welfare, health and judicial services. Critics of the county charge that at least some of the projects are unnecessary, serving merely to please department heads and give the supervisors 'goodies they can take back to their districts.'"

Most capital projects are built without voter approval, frequently after citizens have refused to give the necessary two-thirds vote to issue general obligation bonds. When bond issues are rejected, supervisors find other sources of money. At least one supervisor was uneasy about the extent of construction going on without voter approval. "The first 20 times or so (proposals came up for funding without a bond referendum), I voted against them." But then his district wanted a new county building and the only way to get it was by building without seeking voter approval. "After that," (the supervisor) says, "I couldn't say no to the others."[5]

In Texas counties the tradition of a commissioner's serving his district has been institutionalized in the county budget. The county judge, elected at large as mentioned previously, serves with four commissioners elected from precincts. Each of the four has full authority for road and bridge construction and maintenance in his precinct. To carry out this authority, the county road budget is divided among the commissioners, who spend their portion as they wish. It is typical practice for each commissioner to hire his own road crew, buy his own equipment, and house it in buildings throughout his district. Usually each commissioner develops his own construction program. Little or no effort is made to coordinate plans with colleagues in neighboring precincts.

How can such an obviously inefficient system be perpetuated? The answer is not clear-cut, especially in light of a 1947 state law which permits voters in each county to abolish it and set up a unified road system supervised by a county engineer. Yet the old system flourishes throughout Texas... "probably because most commissioners prefer the existing arrangement and most voters are either sufficiently satisfied or uninformed... there is no strong demand for change."[6]

Logrolling is not confined to counties, of course, it exists in the smallest town, in the U.S. Congress, and in governments of all sizes and levels in-between. Any group which wants something from government has to take advantage of this system to achieve its objectives.

Administrative Officers

About 350 counties, with a combined population of 57,000,000, appoint a manager, comparable to a city manager, to look after day-to-day operations, in order to insure that programs are running smoothly and that county employees are earning their pay.[7] The manager may be called the chief administrative officer (CAO), county administrator, or appointed county executive.

The concept of a hired manager was first proposed by the National Short Ballot Organization (a reform-minded group) in 1911, when Woodrow Wilson was its president.[8] The idea caught on in cities after Dayton hired a manager in 1914; a few counties adopted the plan in the 1920s and '30s, but it has gained the most widespread acceptance since 1950. The number of counties with managers increased 34 percent from 1965 to 1970, and though urban counties were the first to move in this direction, recent years have seen some enthusiastic acceptance in rural areas.[9]

The county manager plan was proposed as a way to make local government more responsive. The originators of the concept believed the governing board should concentrate on policy, leaving the administration to trained managers. The National Short Ballot Organization, the National Municipal League and other early backers were anxious to make local government more businesslike, which could be achieved, in their view, only by removing politicians from the administration of public services. Making sure that the trash was picked up, the school buses ran on time, and the social workers checked on welfare mothers were regarded as technical assignments devoid of politics.

The cities and counties adopting the council-manager plan forty or fifty years ago may have believed that policy making and policy implementation could be separated, but not today. In recent years counties have adopted the plan because their responsibilities have become so complex that it has been impossible for part-time commissioners both to direct county services and to devote proper attention to important policy issues. M.D. Tarshes, former appointed executive of Sacramento County, California put it this way:

The problems posed for county government in California by rapid population growth, with the need to provide major services — welfare, hospitals, roads, public health, airports, land use planning, police protection, fire protection, etc. — appear to have hastened the evolution of the appointed executive plan in order to maintain some measure of control and direction over the administrative process. . . . It has been estimated that the basic functions of county government in California have grown from 22 in 1859 to over 900 today. Los Angeles County, with approximately 40 percent of the state's population, now has an annual budget of in excess of $1 billion. Even those California counties which are in the lower end of the population scale have multi-million dollar annual budgets. Sacramento County, which ranks eighth in size with a population of about 640,000 has an annual budget of slightly over $100 million.[10]

Theoretically county managers are supposed to strengthen their county commission by assuming many of its more routine tasks, giving the commissioners more time for the important issues. The role that many managers play in the decision-making should not be underestimated, however. In practice, while some managers enhance their commissions, there are other who clearly weaken them. On the other hand, managers often use or are used by the governing board for political purposes.

The manager's formal responsibilities vary from state to state. Strong officers are given many responsibilities, including full charge of county departments, hiring and firing right up to the top, the preparation of the budget, ensuring that expenditures are in line with appropriations, and, of great significance, recommending new policies and programs. In short, the strong managers occupy such powerful and far-reaching positions that they are at the forefront of decision-making in their counties, as the Sacramento County organization chart shows. In Los Angeles County, the chief administrative officer is proud that over 95 percent of the actions taken by the board of supervisors concur with his recommendations.[11] "Weak" managers, on the other hand, are hired primarily as staff consultants to the commissioners. They usually do not supervise administrative departments or hire and fire employees.

Managers of any substance, merely by carrying out their assignments, influence political decisions because so many counties are governed by part-time commissions. With commissioners in and out of their courthouse offices for a few hours per week, the man who has full-time charge of government operations, plus the professional knowledge that goes with it, shoulders a great part of the responsibility. News accounts of the budget-making process in Dade County, Florida show how powerful county managers can be. The *Miami Herald* referred to the proposed budget as "the county manager's budget," reporting that "the manager plans to spend tax money" for two new branch libraries, comprehensive planning, a new government center, human resources and other programs, but that most emphasis in the election year budget would be on "three issues that arouse the hottest local concern — law and order, health, and the environment."[12] No matter how powerful he becomes, however, he would never upstage his politician-employers in the public eye. In fact, the Dade County manager was applauded for his political savvy by recommending cuts in the portion of the election year budget to be financed by the property tax while proposing a $22.8 million increase in spending on constituent oriented programs.[13] Clearly, what is good politics for the county commissioners is also good politics for the manager.

Managers are not the only personnel with decision-making powers. Heads of departments also can exercise tremendous influence over county programs, even in counties having professional managers, because they, like the manager, establish good working relationships with the commissioner in charge of their department. In many counties, commissioners operate under a committee system, with committees corresponding to the various administrative depart-

81

COUNTY OF SACRAMENTO – ORGANIZATION CHART

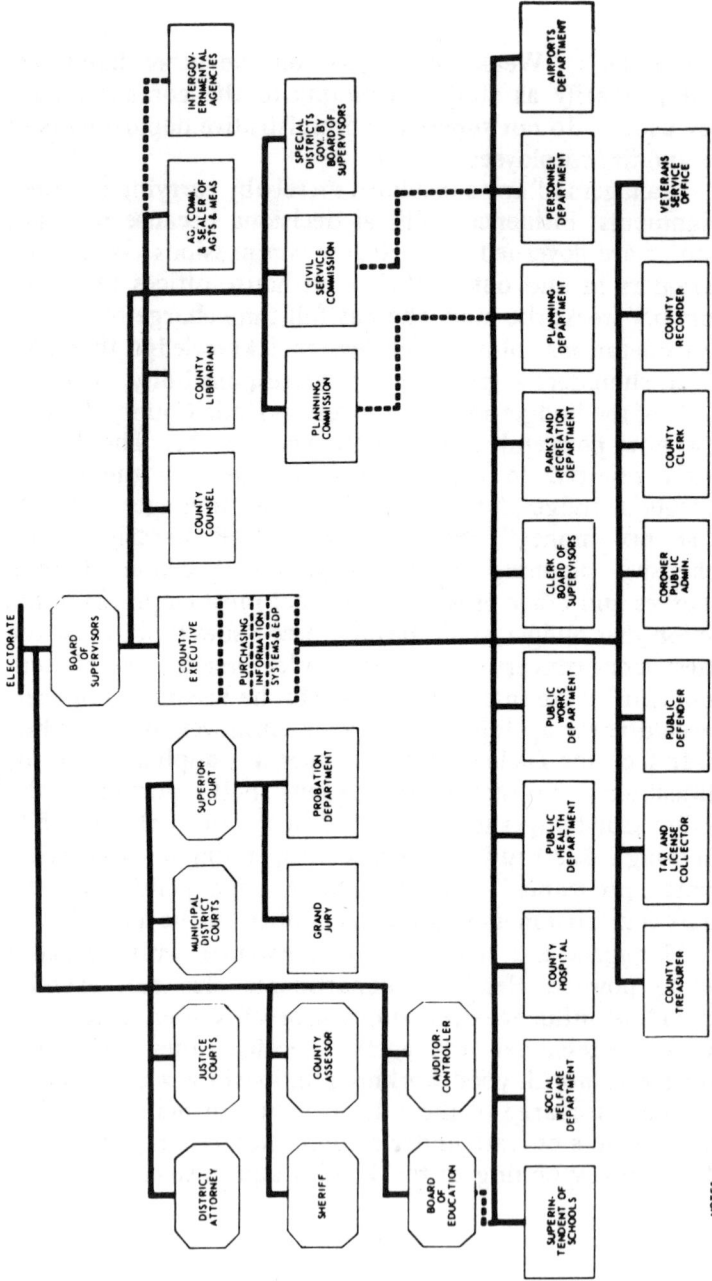

ELECTORATE

BOARD OF SUPERVISORS

COUNTY EXECUTIVE

PURCHASING, INFORMATION SYSTEMS & EDP

INTERGOVERNMENTAL AGENCIES

AG. COMM. & SEALER OF AGTS & MEAS

COUNTY LIBRARIAN

COUNTY COUNSEL

SPECIAL DISTRICTS GOV. BY BOARD OF SUPERVISORS

CIVIL SERVICE COMMISSION

PLANNING COMMISSION

MUNICIPAL DISTRICT COURTS

SUPERIOR COURT

JUSTICE COURTS

DISTRICT ATTORNEY

PROBATION DEPARTMENT

GRAND JURY

COUNTY ASSESSOR

SHERIFF

AUDITOR-CONTROLLER

BOARD OF EDUCATION

SUPERINTENDENT OF SCHOOLS

AIRPORTS DEPARTMENT

PERSONNEL DEPARTMENT

PLANNING DEPARTMENT

PARKS AND RECREATION DEPARTMENT

CLERK BOARD OF SUPERVISORS

PUBLIC WORKS DEPARTMENT

PUBLIC HEALTH DEPARTMENT

COUNTY HOSPITAL

SOCIAL WELFARE DEPARTMENT

VETERANS SERVICE OFFICE

COUNTY RECORDER

COUNTY CLERK

CORONER PUBLIC ADMIN.

PUBLIC DEFENDER

TAX AND LICENSE COLLECTOR

COUNTY TREASURER

NOTES

INDICATES LINE OF DIRECT AUTHORITY THROUGH APPOINTMENT OR ELECTION

INDICATES LINE OF INDIRECT AUTHORITY, COORDINATION AND OR ADVISORY RELATIONSHIP

INDICATES ELECTIVE OFFICIALS

Source: County of Sacramento

ments and the committee chairman responsible for the activities of that department.

According to one journalist, decisions are often made by department heads who propose, the manager who approves, and the board of commissioners which orders. As part of the process, department heads engage in their own forms of lobbying, trying quietly behind the scenes to line up votes among commissioners for projects they believe should be undertaken.

It was by this process, claims two reporters, that Jefferson Boulevard in Los Angeles County was adorned with $74,000 worth of plastic trees.[14] In this case, the supervisor responsible for the road department was also the supervisor of the district involved. Over the years, the head of the road department had developed a close relationship with the supervisor; the supervisor, in turn, allowed the department head to run his office as he saw fit, with the understanding that he would do what he could to help his supervisor politically.

The plastic tree episode began early in 1971, when the residents of Jefferson Boulevard wanted landscaping on the center divider. The road administrator thought normal planting was impossible because a storm drain was located only 18 inches under the divider, so to overcome the problem, he proposed experimentation with artificial landscaping. His supervisor accepted the recommendation; the chief administrative officer made the item a routine part of the agenda for the supervisors' weekly meeting, and the other supervisors went along, as was customary. The county proceeded to let a contract for the plastic trees. But the process hit a snag: environmentalists expressed outrage at the "planting" of plastic foliage. According to local observers:

"The outrage. . . astonished everyone at the Hall of Administration. At no point in the process had there been any objection to the idea, any hearings on it, any debate about it; no one in the 'county family' had had any idea that plastic trees might be controversial."[15]

As one journalist evaluating the changes in his county

because of the new manager system discovered, the most obvious difference the administrator makes is the aura of professionalism he lends to county business. He is in the position to take an overview on county politics and to see the practical relationships between decisions and their consequences, which the part-time commissioners do not. His professional training enables him to deal with problems in sophisticated ways. But he is not directly responsible to the electorate; his power may give him great influence, especially if he is adept at working behind the scenes, but dissatisfied citizens cannot vote him out, even if they recognize his role in the state of affairs. They do vote for the commissioners, who in turn can put heat on the manager; so the manager quickly finds himself walking the tightrope between personal initiative and the acceptance he has to have by the commissioners and the voters who hold the power behind them.

Independently Elected Officials

In most counties the commissioners share their power with various commissions, boards, special districts, and the offices responsible for state mandated functions, which are usually elective and sometimes appointed by the state, such as the sheriff, clerk or recorder, coroner, treasurer, auditor and so on. Some counties elect as many as eleven "row officers." These officers are under no obligation to work with the commissioners or the county manager. In the modern county, however, this is often academic because their jobs are not policy oriented and often not even necessary. The position remains and the office is filled because the state constitution says it must be. Usually noncontroversial in nature, the turnover in these offices is small, and there is little demand for professional qualifications.

Some are vital to the health of the county, however, the assessor and the treasurer being good examples. Elected in about 87 percent of the nation's counties, together they determine how much income the county will raise each year, within statutory restrictions set by the state. Both jobs are highly technical, but by 1968 only four states had established statewide qualifications for eligibility.[16] In other states any persons meeting the age and residency requirements could run for either office. Fortunately there are meetings the newly elected officials can attend to learn some of the skills, and the International Association of Assessing Officers is eager to help. Nevertheless, the problems which remain for the nonprofessional are obvious.

Essentially the assessor is responsible for "discovering," which means listing and appraising, property for ad valorem taxation, a crucial function because the real property tax is the primary source of revenues for most counties. The assessor maintains a current record of property values and appraises property periodically. This last function can, and often does, result in public outrage, especially when housing values climb because of inflation, housing shortages, or as the direct result of some county policy. Montgomery County, Maryland, where housing values have skyrocketed, in part because of the sewer moratorium mentioned in Chapter 3, is a good example.

In Montgomery County the assessor is appointed by the state, yet he re-evaluates one-third of all Montgomery County taxable property each year. In 1973 the value of one home was increased by 42.4 percent, another by 30 percent and one by 12 percent. Of the 62,000 property owners affected, over 4000 protested their increases, 644 successfully obtained reversals and lower assessments for their property, usually because they were able to prove that their houses had structural defects; wet basements, cracked foundations, bad topography, or adverse environmental factors, such as a proposed six-lane highway adjacent to the property. Due to the reassessments, the county income will increase substantially — enough to avoid a tax rate increase. Nevertheless the elected county executive,

85

the council, and the public are involved in a controversy about the costs of government, tax rates and exorbitant property values. The fact remains, the county council and the elected executive, who have full responsibility for meeting the financial obligations of the county, have no control over the assessment process — the formula used to re-evaluate property — nor do they control how accurately and swiftly the reassessments will take place.

Where the assessor's responsibilities stop, the treasurer takes over. The assessor may find it his duty to compute the market value on which the taxpayer must pay, but the treasurer actually computes the tax bill, sends it out, and collects it if taxpayers are uncooperative.

In most counties the treasurer controls the county's cash and securities, though the county commission still decides how the money will be spent. The treasurer also invests idle funds, invests in long-term trusts and other funds, manages the long-term debt and borrows money for the short term. Often these duties are carried out by an official who has no statutory obligations to work or consult with the commission or executive. Instead, the treasurer, like the auditor, looks to the state constitution, state laws, and his financial colleagues at the state level for direction. The county governing board takes over, however, in setting the tax rate and drafting the budget.

The office of sheriff is another sensitive position. In many counties, including highly urbanized ones such as the consolidated government of Jacksonville-Duval County, Florida, the sheriff is elected. The only formal control the governing board has is the budget allotment. Yet confused voters may hold the commissioners responsible for crime in the streets or wonder why the sheriff never seems to have a law enforcement background or any clear-cut knowledge of criminology.

History is the reason so many counties have elected non-professionals supervising the county jail, maintaining public records, and determining causes of death. When county government was taking form in many states, the Jacksonian idea of direct democracy was popular. Provisions were made in state constitutions for the direct election of county officials who were, after all, supposed to carry out state responsibilities at the local level. The last two states to join the union took a more modern approach to local government and several counties in Alaska and Hawaii do not elect any row officers. Unfortunately many outmoded provisions and laws remain, while the needs of counties and the concepts of democracy have changed. A few states are abolishing unneeded "row officers" or establishing professional requirements, but progress is slow because of the political strength of the "row officers" themselves. In countless instances they have generated enough statewide support to defeat legislation which threatens the existence of their jobs.

County Executive Form

Although decentralization of authority is characteristic of most counties, a handful of them — 50 to be exact* — have reorganized their governing bodies, separated the legislative from the administrative function, and established the position of elected county executive. Unlike the presiding officer of most county commissions, the executive is elected at large, usually for a four year term, and is given enough responsibility and authority to provide leadership to the government. The position also has symbolic significance — the executive, similar to a mayor or a governor, represents county government to most citizens. He is, in their minds, the head of the government.

---

*Includes consolidated city-counties classified as counties by the National Association of Counties. Three New York counties — Chautauqua, Albany and Chemung — will have a council-executive government effective November 1974, bringing the number to 53.

Counties with executives, while scattered throughout 18 states, are especially popular in Maryland, New York, and Hawaii. Of Maryland's 23 counties, including the city of Baltimore,* seven have executives; all four counties in Hawaii have executives, and ten in New York have them (to be increased by three in 1974). Most choosing this type of organization are densely populated, having from 100,000 to 600,000 residents.

Although one or two counties have restricted their executives to little more than ceremonial roles, the majority have granted substantial powers to influence county policy. One of the greatest advantages of the plan is greater centralization of administration, which is the full-time job of the executive. He proposes programs, drafts both an operating and a capital budget, and takes full charge of the day-to-day operations of government. Usually assisted by a manager who is his right-hand man, he appoints his own department heads. The council is the legislative body, proposing programs and ordinances of its own, but it also acts on the executive's ideas and authorizes his budget. Executives may veto council actions, and the council, in turn, has the power to override the veto. Under the executive plan the lines of authority are supposed to be clear-cut. The executive and the council both can generate policies and make decisions, but the executive alone takes charge of delivering the services and giving life to the programs. Or so it seems. However, power is more fragmented than one might guess. Many departments may continue to be led by independently elected officers; administrative tasks may be in the hands of semi-autonomous commissions and special districts. As the organization chart of Baltimore County, Maryland shows, the executive has control over many services — fire, public works, recreation and so on — but others,

*Baltimore City, located outside of Baltimore County, is treated as both a city and a county by the Maryland constitution.

GOVERNMENTAL ORGANIZATION OF BALTIMORE COUNTY

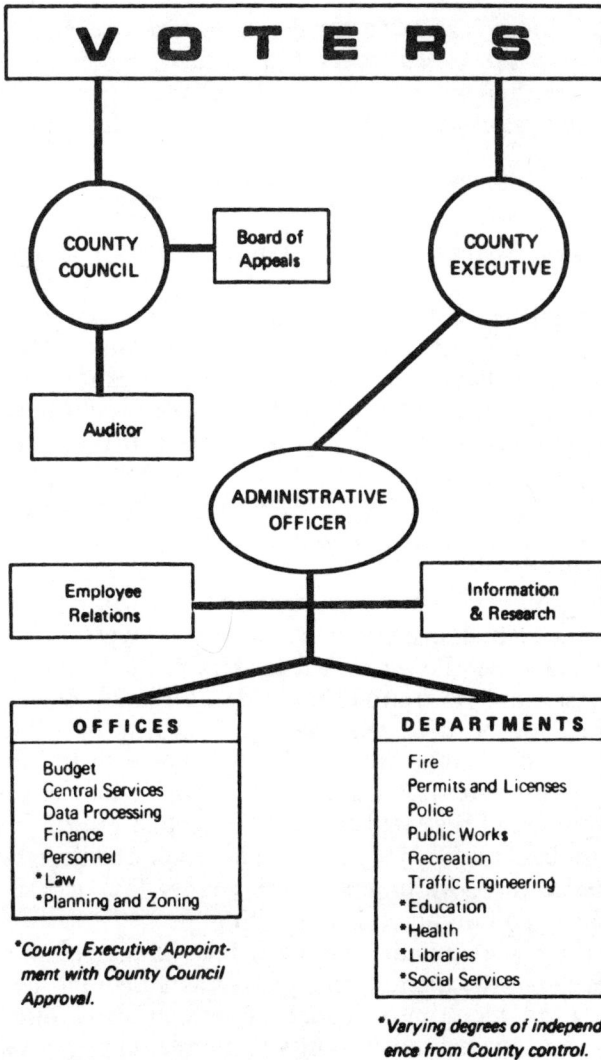

VOTERS

COUNTY COUNCIL — Board of Appeals

COUNTY EXECUTIVE

Auditor

ADMINISTRATIVE OFFICER

Employee Relations

Information & Research

OFFICES

Budget
Central Services
Data Processing
Finance
Personnel
*Law
*Planning and Zoning

*County Executive Appointment with County Council Approval.

DEPARTMENTS

Fire
Permits and Licenses
Police
Public Works
Recreation
Traffic Engineering
*Education
*Health
*Libraries
*Social Services

*Varying degrees of independence from County control.

AGENCIES NOT DIRECTLY CONTROLLED BY CHARTER:

Board of Supervisors of Elections
Board of Liquor License Commissioners
Supervisor of Assessments
Appeal Tax Court
Baltimore County Revenue Authority

County Surveyor
Cooperative Extension Service
County Judicial System—Circuit Court
Orphans' Court
Clerk of Circuit Court

Register of Wills
State's Attorney
County Sheriff
Trial Magistrates
People's Court

Source: *America's County Today,* NACO, Washington, D.C. 1973.

especially those mandated by the state, are not directly responsible to the executive or the council. Even the finest county governments are the result of a long evolution of change and adjustment, the results of which are only partly rational.

Montgomery County: The Evolution of a Local Government[17]

Montgomery County, Maryland, a large urban suburb of Washington, D.C., is located not far from Baltimore. It is one of the most affluent counties in the United States, a place where good government is a tradition. But it would be a mistake to think of it as a unified government entity; it is a montage of governments, developed partly by design, partly by reactions to immediate needs. Modern in some respects, outmoded in others, it can be understood only from the perspective of history.

Montgomery County was organized in 1776. For most of its life it has had a government structure typical of rural agricultural areas. Power over local affairs was vested in the state legislature. Its tranquil countryside remained virtually untouched by the Civil War and the conflicts of industrial revolution which followed. But in the 20th century, people started to migrate from the wealthy northwest section of Washington, and the great explosion of urban growth began. Their numbers rapidly increasing, a new type of citizen began to influence the government of the county, but it was well established and initially resistant to change.

As the new population began to form in a series of communities along the district line, there was a demand for services not available from the county. Problems arose which the local government had no authority to handle. In response, the state of Maryland created two large bicounty units (in combination with the neighboring Prince Georges County):

(1) The Washington Suburban Sanitary Commission,

1917 — In reaction to requests from the District of Columbia this agency was designed to plan for and control the development of sewage facilities for a bi-county area. The explosion of suburban home sewage systems was creating threatening pollution problems for many streams and rivers in the area.

(2) The Maryland National Capital Park and Planning Commission, 1927 — Created by the state, this agency was to develop a comprehensive land development plan to preserve stream valley parkland. It would become the county's central planning office, though hardly a county agency.

The county was to collect taxes in support of these institutions, and although it had little power over them, members of both commissions considered themselves responsible to the state legislature. Ever larger and more powerful, these agencies exist today.

Their establishment was a precedent for the tendency to establish separate government agencies to handle specific problems, rather than vesting such functions in the county government. In time there would be an extensive list of organizations coexisting if not competing with the county. In addition to the Montgomery County government and the two bi-county commissions, there now exist:

Three fully incorporated municipalities
Eight towns with some governmental powers
Ten special service districts with power to levy taxes
Sixteen independent fire departments, an elected fire board and five fire districts
Six additional major tax districts
Four parking lot districts
An elected board of education and a semi-independent public school system
Montgomery County Community College
Washington Suburban Transit Commission

The Housing Authority
The Revenue Authority

The new citizens flooding to the county were well paid professionals, politically informed and articulate. They came to the Washington area in the expansion of the federal government created by the New Deal. They were a stark contrast to the landed gentry and the farmers whom they found in the county, and the issues were soon joined. City oriented and believers in strong executive leadership, the newcomers resented the lax system of government in Montgomery County. A part-time board of five commissioners was responsible for day-to-day operations, serving as both legislators and executives. Meeting irregularly, each commissioner was out for the interests of his own district, and decisions were made by political horsetrading. More important, most authority remained with the state legislature, which met every two years, deciding even such things as salary changes and actions concerning key personnel, let alone the issuance of bonds or the reorganization of departments. Long-range fiscal planning was impossible.

In the 1930s there was a nationwide movement toward a "new county" concept, with strong executive leadership and a local charter, which bore fruit in Montgomery County in 1948. A home rule charter established a council/manager form of government. Day-to-day administration was assigned to a professional hired by a council of elected officials. The council served both as a legislative branch and as overseer of the manager. For the first time administration was shielded from the traditional horsetrading and technical personnel were brought in to cope with the county's rapidly developing urban problems. A new merit system and a civil service commission for government personnel were established, and a finance department was organized to improve tax assessment and capital budgeting procedures. Open hearings for legislative programs were instituted, and a revised county code was established.

A streamlined, more efficient form of government was

achieved, but a critical gap remained. The sanitary commission and the capital planning commission were left essentially intact, and their vital planning functions remained outside the aegis of the local government because the state legislature was unwilling to submerge them into the "new county."

The charter worked well for over a decade, but the 1960s, which doubled the county's population, brought drastic new pressures. Air pollution, race relations, public transportation, urban renewal, public housing, a horrendous controversy over commercial zoning, all brought demands for a broader political perspective and an understanding of the interrelated issues of the metropolitan area. The county was in the grips of an unprecedented traffic and population density which was highly visible to its citizens.

In 1968 a new charter was adopted to combine political leadership with professional administration and to create a government more responsive to the overall needs of the people.

An elected county executive was created to bring political and public focus to administration.

Political responsibility was vested in a legislative body, a seven member council of part-time elected officials (though presently many members work full time).

The position of chief administrative officer was established to handle the day-to-day administration.

The new form of government was based on a clear separation of powers. It addressed fragmentation indirectly by establishing a six year capital expenditures plan for a broad range of agencies within the county and by including the budgets for those agencies in the county's annual budgeting process.

Montgomery County is entering the 1970s as a community and a government which have undergone a drastic metamorphosis from the rural nature at the outset of the century. Yet many of the old issues and subdivisions of authority remain. While it grapples with the most modern of problems, the county is still a fragmented, multiple government, its splintered authority no more apparent than in the vital process of planning for future growth.

The government must make the right choices about growth if the citizens are to have the community they want for the future. In something so complex as a metropolitan suburb of over half a million, arriving at the right choices requires long-range planning that, in fact, acts as a framework for careful coordination of government policy. Zoning must result in the proper balance and location of commercial and industrial construction, apartments, recreation and park land, and single-family housing. Sewer lines must be developed in line with zoning policy, and there must be adequate development of waste treatment facilities. The transportation system must expand to handle and distribute traffic flow according to the growth patterns. All policies must combine to develop the kind of community the citizens seek, at the same time maintaining the strong financial footing of the government (Montgomery County is presently rated at AAA in the bond markets). For planning to work this effectively, there must be a flow from planning... to the establishment of policy... to the creation of legislation... to the implementation of programs... the results of which feed back into... planning.

How does it work in Montgomery County? Overall planning is the responsibility of the Montgomery County Planning Board which is comprised of half of the ten commissioners of the Maryland National Capital Park and Planning Commission, the state appointed, independent planning authority established in 1927. The Montgomery half of the commission reports directly to the county council for planning purposes, but is funded by the county executive from county tax revenues. The council is responsible for legislation, the county executive for implementation of the legislation and the day-to-day supervision of the agencies which execute programs. No one person or authority is responsible for the coordination of this planning process to insure that planning properly reflects the results of the expensive and large-scale planning efforts, that the legislation effectively enacts the results of planning and policy, or that implementation effectively brings the process into action, or that the realities and results of implementing programs are fed back into the planning process to make it realistic and responsive to the developments taking place in the community. In fact, political rivalry has resulted in so much bickering and faulty communication among the planning board, the council and the county executive, that there is no assurance the millions spent annually on long-range planning have the needed impact on the governmental process.

To make matters worse, sewer lines are developed, maintained and financed by the independent Washington Suburban Sanitary Commission, though the county executive has the nominal responsibility for long-range planning for sewer development. The planning board is responsible for planning the county's roads, but the executive's department of transportation, which has its own planning section, actually builds the roads and maintains over 1400 miles of local streets. At the same time the state department of transportation builds and maintains the nearly 300 miles of major highways in the county. The state highway administration establishes 5-year and 20-year road projections for the county, which are reviewed and commented on by the executive and the council, though final power for their approval rests with the county delegation of state legislators.

This story of fractured authority and responsibility among state capital, county executive, county council, and independent local agencies is repeated in public education, drugs, health, the Washington metropolitan subway system and on and on. No one would advocate the concentration of all powers for these massive and complex local operations in one individual or department, but it doesn't take more than common sense to realize that the present system cannot work efficiently.

Through its history Montgomery County has moved

steadily and progressively toward more unified and effective local government, bringing it to the forefront of counties all over the country. Yet its problems with fragmentation indicate that local government needs further reform to confront the future effectively.

Recruiting Candidates

The way authority is distributed throughout the county is important in figuring out who will make decisions and how they will be made, but the rules about recruiting candidates for commissioner, executive, sheriff and all the other offices, and then electing them, also play a part.

How do people become county commissioners? They win elections of course, but even here there are exceptions. There are some pre-Revolution vestiges in Georgia and South Carolina where, in 19 counties the governor appoints some or all governing board members. In twelve Massachusetts counties the board is nominated by the grand jury and appointed by the judge of the superior court.[18]

But for a majority of counties the real story begins months or even years before the general election, when the hopefuls begin to learn about government, line up supporters, and then in most cases win a primary election to be nominated, formally, to run as a candidate in the general election.

In 1922 Harry S. Truman was elected to the three-member county court, the governing body of Jackson County, Missouri. He ran with the backing of Tom Pendergast, leader of the political machine which dominated Kansas City and Jackson County from the 1890s to 1939. Pendergast supported Truman for practical reasons. From 1918 through the early 1920s, the political boss had competition from other Democratic party leaders over control of the county. The infighting resulted in strong-arm tactics, violence and generally unfavorable public reaction which threatened a Republican takeover in the 1922 election. To appease the reform-minded electorate, Pendergast relinquished some special favors he had previously granted to contractors in Jackson County, and supported some "good government" candidates. As a result of Truman's election, "all observers seemed to agree that the old style of corrupt practices... were stopped at this time."[19] In 1930, Pendergast backed Truman for the post of presiding judge of the Jackson County court, and in 1934, when Truman was hoping for party support to run for county collector, the machine selected him as a candidate for the U.S. Senate.

Years later and many miles from Missouri, Spiro Agnew first became involved in politics when, on the advice of a friend, he switched his party affiliation from Democrat to Republican because there were fewer young lawyers to compete with in the Baltimore County Republican Party.[20] In 1957 the new party allegiance paid off — Agnew was appointed a minority member of the Baltimore County Board of Zoning Appeals, and later he became its chairman. After assuming a more active role in the Republican party and working diligently on the Baltimore County home rule charter movement, Agnew was elected the Baltimore County Executive in 1962. Four years later, with the backing of the Republican party, he was elected governor of Maryland and finally, in 1968, he became vice president of the United States.

Not all county officeholders go on to state and national positions (although many ex-county officials are now sitting in state houses, state legislatures, and the U.S. Congress), and not all of them enter politics the ways Truman and Agnew did. For many candidates or would-be candidates, support of a political party is necessary, as in the cases of Truman and Agnew; for others it is not as important. State constitutional and statutory provisions determine the role of political parties and the requirements for eligibility of candidates. In most states, those who want to be county officials must first be

97

nominated through direct primary elections, which are non-partisan in some states and partisan in others. In Washington state, for example, those aspiring to be commissioners seek the nomination from their district in a partisan primary. The nominees of each party then run — at large in the general election. By contrast, a 1965 Wisconsin law stipulates that county officers be selected from districts for a two-year term at a nonpartisan election held in the spring. The law further classifies all 72 of the state's counties by population and establishes the maximum size of the governing board for counties in each category.[21] In partisan primaries, voters determine whom the Republicans, Democrats, and other parties will bring out as their candidates. The rules, both formal and informal, concerning who may run in the primary differ from state to state and county to county.

In some counties, committees of both political parties endorse slates of candidates. These slates may be unopposed or may meet competition either from other factions of the parties or from individuals who do not have the backing of any particular group but have met the requirements for getting on the ballot. In other counties, slates are not permitted or simply are not drafted. Running on a slate with other potential nominees is helpful to the political newcomer — it helps advertise his name and associates him with others who may be well-known incumbents or party regulars.

The Electoral Process

Primary elections may be open or closed. In open primaries, voters do not need to declare their allegiance to a political party until they walk into the polling place and request the ballot. In the closed primary, voters must state, usually at the time they register to vote, which party they belong to. When they appear at the polling place, they are given the ballot for the appropriate party. There are several variations of the open and closed primaries which make it easier or more difficult for voters to switch from one party to another.

Primary elections in some states are nonpartisan. In Californian for example, all county officers are elected on nonpartisan ballots. Even in counties with this type of nominating procedure, political parties may play a significant role by urging candidates to run. If political parties do not assume this function, other nonpartisan "political" organizations and interests probably will. In nonpartisan Arlington County, Virginia, for example, the ABC (Arlingtonians for a Better County) has all the trappings of a local Democratic or Republican party at election time.

Winners of primaries have successfully won the first battle — the right to run for county office. In partisan primaries they become their party's official candidate. The next battle is the general election. In many counties where one party is dominant, winning the primary is tantamount to winning the general election. In these areas, intense competition may occur within the dominant party during the primary, and it is in the primary that the officeholder is chosen in fact if not legally. In counties where forces are fairly evenly split, the general election is the payoff.

In the general election, voters of the county may not vote for all the positions on the commission because, in about half of all counties, candidates run from districts to which the voters are restricted.[22] (Some counties have single-member districts; others have multi-member districts and elect several representatives to the governing body.) In most of the rest, voters cast ballots for all governing board seats. (There are numerous variations of the at-large selection method, one of the most common being the requirement that candidates running at large live in particular election districts, such as in Colorado, Florida, Montana, New Mexico and Washington.) Until recently voters in some states, principally Michigan, Wisconsin, New York, Illinois and some parts of New Jersey, selected county governing board members indirectly when they selected officials of municipalities, townships, or other subunits of the county. These local officials, usually the mayor or township manager, automatically became county supervisors, and the county was governed by a loose confederation of officials who owed their first allegiance to another local government. U.S. Supreme Court apportionment decisions have forced reorganization of the supervisor form, and some counties have given up the system altogether. The supervisor system did not meet the one man-one vote test because each municipality within the county sent the same number of representatives to the county board, irrespective of the population of the town. In Michigan the supervisor plan was abandoned, and now county commissioners are elected from districts. In New Jersey, the large county boards were dismantled and replaced by seven-member commissions elected at large. In Wisconsin, as mentioned, county board members are now chosen from legislative districts of nearly equal population. New York experienced a variety of approaches. Of the state's 57 counties, 38 now elect county legislators from single-member districts, multi-member districts or a combination of the two. Three counties have not yet reapportioned. The remaining 21 counties still select supervisors from municipalities but each one has voting strength based on the number of constituents he represents.[23] Nassau County is a case in point. A total of 130 votes is distributed among six supervisors as shown below. (The town of Hempstead contains 55 percent of the county population and is represented by two supervisors; each of the other municipalities has one representative.)

Municipality	Representatives	Majority Vote
Hempstead	2	70 (35 each)
Oyster Bay	1	32
North Hempstead	1	23
Long Beach	1	3
Glen Cove	1	2

100

Each supervisor has voting power roughly equivalent to the population he represents, such that each member of the county board could cast a deciding vote the same percentage of the time as his constituency would be able to.

The way commissioners are elected, from districts or at large, and the size and number of electoral districts, may seem trivial, but experienced politicians feel that these factors have significant influence. The boundaries of election districts often decide which interests have the best opportunity to win, and boundaries can usually be drawn to favor one interest, although the results are not always predictable. When schools in the Detroit section of Wayne County, Michigan were decentralized in 1969 by setting up eight neighborhood school districts, each with a five-member elected board, and a city-wide board composed of the chairman of each neighborhood board plus five members elected at large, community controversy developed over drawing the neighborhood district lines. Black groups wanted to ensure black control over black schools and sought designation of some predominantly black districts; white conservatives wanted the same thing to avoid busing; others wanted districts with mixes of blacks and whites to ensure integration. Finally, district boundaries were drawn which officials thought would result in four districts controlled by blacks and four by whites. But this did not happen in the first neighborhood school board elections. Blacks won a majority in only two districts, and only three blacks served on the city-wide board — the smallest proportion in 15 years. Two represented regional boards and one was elected at large.[24] Nevertheless there are many approaches, such as concentrating most blacks in one or two districts and whites in the rest, or diluting the black vote through several districts. The central city can be split into several districts, each with a suburban component, to insure that the central city residents would usually be outvoted by suburbanites, or the districts could be drawn in favor of the central city. Such is the case in Milwaukee County, Wisconsin where 13 of the 24 electoral

101

districts represent the central city, six represent mixed city and suburban areas and the remainig five represent the suburbs.[25] The possibilities for biasing elections through districting are numerous.

The number of districts is important because it determines, in large measure, the accessibility of commissioners. The median size of elected governing boards with district divisions is four. The relatively small number of county commissioners, especially in densely populated counties, means that each commissioner represents thousands of citizens. In Contra Costa County, California each member of the five-member board of supervisors represents about 100,000 citizens; in Alameda County, the ratio of representatives to constituents is 1 to 250,000, and in Los Angeles County it is roughly one board member to every 1,500,000.[26] A few large districts or at-large elections often make it difficult for minority groups to be heard.[27] Furthermore, the costs of campaigning increase with the size of the electoral district, giving incumbents a clear advantage. It has been estimated that the cost of running for Los Angeles County supervisor in a contest election is from $200,000 to $300,000. The turnover among supervisors in this county has been quite low. Until the death of one governing board member in 1971, there had been no new faces on the board in 14 years; the deceased man's successor was the twentieth person to serve on the board since 1913.[28]

With the current emphasis on small government and direct, widespread citizen involvement, having three or four persons represent hundreds of thousands or even millions of constituents seems headed for trouble, and a handful of counties have taken steps to decentralize by providing more opportunities for county officials to meet and talk with their constituents. Usually this takes the form of — neighborhood hearings and "meet your commissioner" sessions, opening "little county courthouses" and setting up one-stop multi-service centers in various parts of the county. Dade County, Florida, for example, opened the South Dade Government Center in 1972, in order to make it easier for citizens to pick up marriage licenses, pay taxes, contact officials about problems and take care of routine matters. Now, instead of driving to the county courthouse, residents living near the center can walk or take a quick car trip and handle their affairs. Most county departments are represented at the government center so citizens can contact officials about problems as diverse as zoning decisions, pollution control, consumer protection and juvenile problems.[29] Decentralization has been a big city issue, but as counties take on urban problems and as citizens become more vocal, they also can be expected to take a good look at decentralization.

Almost everyone who has written about county government and many who have worked in it condemn the way the power to make decisions and to take action is distributed. The "leaderless" commission form inhibits the swift, decisive action needed to solve contemporary problems, one reason the executive-council is so widely heralded. The dominant theme of county reform literature is the vast potential just waiting to be tapped if only the yoke of archaic governmental structure can be lifted.[30] Why is this taking so long to happen? In part, because the old system is embedded in state constitutional and statutory provisions which are always so difficult to change, partially because state legislators are cautious about increasing the powers of their local governments, and partially because incumbent county officials know how to work the old system, despite its drawbacks.

Nevertheless, county governments are reorganizing. Many states now allow counties to adopt forms of government they design themselves, in the form of a charter and public incorporation. At least 19 states now permit counties to have charters, and 33 of the 58 charter counties (and city-counties)

103

have reorganized with a county executive and a council.* (A few more counties such as Milwaukee County, Wisconsin and New Castle County, Delaware operate under the executive form without charter, but with permission granted through state law.) By granting counties the authority to adopt charters, the state reverses the Dillon Rule and supplants it with the so-called Fordham Principle. Unlike the Dillon Rule which essentially says that the county is a creature of the state, authorized to do only what the state explicitly says it may or must do, the Fordham Principle allows counties to exercise any governmental function not prohibited by state constitution or general laws. By granting the authority to operate under a charter, the state officially views counties as local governments in their own rights, not merely regional appendages of the state house.

Other states allow counties flexibility in organizing their governments, but fall short of delegating full home rule powers. The 1972 New Jersey Optional Forms Bill gives counties power to reorganize under one of four alternatives: elected county executive, strong manager, elected supervisor, or board president. In the same year the Utah constitution was amended authorizing counties to choose one of twelve governmental structures which can be adopted through one of four different procedures.

As urbanization continues, counties face ever-increasing responsibilities. States are likely to look to the county as a means for dealing with regional problems, as well as local ones. Increasingly, states will recognize that counties need more centralized authority, and more counties, given the opportunity, will adopt the executive plan of government.

---

*The number of charter counties will increase to 61 and the number of charter counties with elected executives will increase to 36 in November 1974 when the charters of Albany, Chautauqua and Chemung Counties, New York become effective.

Notes

1. Banfield, Edward C. and James Q. Wilson, *City Politics,* (New York: Vintage Books, 1963), p. 79.

2. National Association of Counties staff, December 1973.

3. Anderson, James, Richard Murray, and Edward Farley, *Texas Politics: An Introduction,* (New York: Harper and Row Publishers, 1971), p. 254.

4. Abernethy, Bob and Art White, "The Invisible Growth Machine," *Los Angeles Times West Magazine,* May 28, 1972, p. 15.

5. *Ibid.,* p. 7-15.

6. Anderson, Murray and Farley, *op. cit.,* p. 256.

7. National Association of Counties staff, November 1973.

8. Banfield and Wilson, *op. cit.,* p. 168.

9. *From America's Counties Today,* (Washington, D.C.: National Association of Counties, 1973), p. 15.

10. Tarshes, M.D., "The Appointed County Executive," in *Guide to County Organization and Management,* (Washington, D.C.: National Association of Counties, 1968), p. 162.

11. Abernethy and White, *op. cit.,* p. 15.

12. *The Miami Herald,* Thursday, June 1, 1972, p. C5.

13. *Ibid.,* p. C1.

14. Abernethy and White, *op. cit.,* p. 10.

15. *Ibid.*

16. *Guide to County Organization and Management,* (Washington, D.C.: National Association of Counties, 1968), p. 254.

17. Drawn from "Montgomery County at the Mid-Million Mark" to be published by Montgomery County, Maryland in 1974.

18. Jones, Victor, Jean Gansel and George F. Howe,

"County Government Organization and Services," in *1972 Municipal Yearbook,* (Washington, D.C.: International City Management Association, 1972), p. 212.

19. Murphy, Thomas P., *Metropolitics and the Urban County,* (Washington, D.C.: Washington National Press, 1970), p. 72.

20. *The Washington Post,* Thursday, October 11, 1973, p. A1.

21. Donoghue, James R., *The Local Government System of Wisconsin,* (Reprinted from the 1968 *Wisconsin Blue Book* published by the state of Wisconsin), p. 24.

22. Advisory Commission on Intergovernmental Relations, *Profile of County Government,* (Washington, D.C.: U.S. Government Printing Office, 1972), p. 17.

23. "Reapportionment of Local Government Legislative Bodies," Information Bulletin #23, June 1973, State of New York Office for Local Government.

24. Torrence, Susan W., *Super City-Home Town, U.S.A.,* (New York: Praeger, 1974).

25. Donoghue, *Ibid.,* p. 26.

26. Jones, Gansel and Howe, *op. cit.*

27. *Ibid.*

28. Abernethy and White, *op. cit.*

29. Torrence, *op. cit.*

30. See: President's Commission on Urban Problems, *Building the American City* (Washington, D.C.: U.S. Government Printing Office, 1968), p. 237; Committee for Economic Development, *Reshaping Government in Metropolitan Areas,* (New York: The Committee, 1970); Council of State Governments, *The States and the Metropolitan Problem,* (The Council, 1956); Robert Warren, *Government in Metropolitan Areas: A Reappraisal of Fractionated Political Organization,* (Davis, California: Institute of Government, 1966); and Herbert Sydney Duncombe, *County Government in America,* (Washington, D.C.: National Association of Counties Research Foundation, 1966).

5. Employees and the Growth of Public Unions

Some Characteristics of Public Employment

Each workday 75,000 employees report to the Los Angeles County government. They provide welfare services to nearly two million persons, assess two million parcels of land and 230,000 businesses and operate the largest hospital system in the United States, among a multitude of assignments. Some even nurture the 100,000 camellias at Descanso Gardens or clean the largest Tyrannosaurus Rex skull on record.[1] All of these people work on all of these assignments, theoretically, to carry out policies set by five men elected to the county board of supervisors.

Most counties aren't this big, but when all 3000 are lumped together it's clear that, nationwide, county government is big business. Well over a million people with hundreds of employment classifications work on thousands of different kinds of jobs.[2] More than 70 percent of the typical county operating budget goes to salaries.[3] These figures are indicative of the expansion of jobs and personnel rosters at all levels of government. By 1970 one-sixth of the nation's labor force worked for a government, exclusive of the military.[4]

The ratio of public to private civilian workers increased

from one out of ten in 1950 to one out of eight in 1960 to the current ratio of one to six.[5] Since World War II, three out of every ten new jobs were government positions. Despite the feeling that the federal government is expanding by leaps and bounds, the figures show that state and local government employment has clearly outstripped it. Close to 80 percent of the 12½ million public employees work for a state or local government, and local governments employ about seven million of these.

The one million-plus county employees are the service arm of their commissioners, and in 50 counties with an elected chief executive, they are hired to carry out the policies of the governing body, to make sure services are adequate, programs are effective and that government in general runs smoothly. This assignment implies that employees suggest as well as implement improvements in present operations, outlining new programs which might be necessary. At the highest level most top county administrators undoubtedly help form county policies regarding specific programs. But employees also are concerned about their pay, their working conditions, and how they are treated by their employers, and their efforts in these areas have affected county budgets, management practices and personnel policies.

Most commissioners work at county business only part time, which gives employees an edge in determining the specifics of policies. Commissioners not only have limited time for supervision, but also lack an intimate knowledge of how the programs work. Thus it is inevitable that county employees not only carry out orders, but play a role in developing new programs. They exercise discretion in the implementation of policy.

Commissioners look to top administrators, especially department heads, to advise them and to recommend policies, which opens the way for these persons, if they so wish, to push their favorite projects, or to withhold information that would be detrimental to their departments and present "facts" in a way that supports their position. They can also generate their own constituency among the general public. Commissioners must rely on the advice and counsel of their administrative personnel because they have little access to other sources of information about their government. Such reliance on professional opinion will probably become greater as the issues of local government become more complex, interrelated and technical.

This growing role of employees in policy making has raised fears that the general public will lose control of their government. Bureaucrats, some argue, are not directly responsible to the general public, yet they make decisions affecting the lives of thousands. Citizens who disagree with the bureaucrats' decisions or actions can complain to the county governing board — but how much actual control does the board have over what the bureaucracy does? Some of these fears may be warranted, but others argue that generally county employees are trying to serve the interests of the majority of citizens. Of course, public interest is always defined from one's own point of view, but most public employees reflect the interests of the constituents they serve. After all, they too are part of the general public.[6]

Most employees tend to identify the public interest with the expectations of their professional peers. They are apt to think that the methods and policies advanced by their colleagues are "right" and in the public interest. They also tend to accept the expectations of their superiors on the job, and to adopt the supervisors' view of the public interest as their own. Finally, in reaching decisions, employees usually try to please the groups in the community which are applying the most pressure. Alert citizens lobby them the same way they lobby elected officials.

The Growing Impact of Unions
and Professional Associations*

Developing policies, carrying out orders and attending to public work consumes most of the energy and time of county employees. But like all members of the labor force, these men and women want pleasant working conditions and modern equipment to carry out their assignments, and they want adequate compensation for their efforts. To realize these goals many employees have followed the example of their counterparts in the private sector. The number of county and city employees carrying union cards is staggering, and their ranks are expected to increase. Excluding teachers, about two million state and local employees, or over one-fourth of the total, are union members.[7] Teachers have been organizing at a tremendous rate. In 1972 about one million teachers belonged to the National Education Association, a professional group, and about 300,000 belonged to its AFL-CIO rival, the American Federation of Teachers.[8]

John F. Kennedy's 1962 executive order making it federal policy to grant recognition to public unions has been the impetus for gains in new membership that have far outstripped union growth in the private sector. From 1962 to

---

*Professional associations while assuming many characteristics of unions (representing members in bargaining with management, pressing for better pay and working conditions, and even calling strikes) differ in one important respect: membership is open to administrators and supervisory personnel. Unions exclude managers, believing that employees' actions are circumscribed if supervisors — members of management — participate in organizations which make demands on them for better working conditions and more pay. Unions are almost exclusively "employment oriented"; associations are also concerned with raising the professionalism of their members.

110

1968 the public employee union and associate membership jumped 136 percent, compared to a five percent increase for private unions.[9] The American Federation of State, County and Municipal Employees, which claims to attract 1000 new members per week, is now 500,000 strong. In the last ten years it has gone from the 19th largest of AFL-CIO unions to the 7th.[10] Membership in public unions and employee associations, exclusive of education, exceeds one-third of the total work force, as compared to the less than 30 percent organization of nonagricultural private employees.[11] As a Nevada county manager put it, "Next to the civil rights movement, the unionization of public employees is one of the greatest social changes occurring throughout the nation."[12]

Unions affect counties and cities alike, and because the issues and tactics are so similar, their statistics are usually lumped together. Even in counties without unions, the movement has had an effect. Clark County, Nevada, for example, which has no unions or even a civil service system, is required to have a grievance board.[13] Although unionism may be more widespread among cities, in 1970 over half of the urban counties had at least one employee organization and some had more than four to deal with.[14] Santa Clara County, California has employees in seven unions or similar professional associations ranging from the County Employees Association to the California Association of Medical Laboratory Technologists; the employees are divided into 14 bargaining units.[15] However, organization is not confined to big counties. Rural, conservative Garrett County, Maryland experienced one of the longest strikes in the history of public unionism, 227 days. One of the results of that strike has implications for the future of all counties. . . in the election which immediately followed, county employees actively campaigned for selected candidates for county commissioner. The board members who were elected immediately reversed the previous policies and recognized the union.

In a geographic pattern similar to private unions, public employees are more organized in the West and Northeast.[16] In

111

South Carolina, where only about 9 percent of the private work force is organized compared to a national average of about 25 to 30 percent, the number of organized public employees is extremely small.[17] Limited numbers do not mean the absence of conflicts, however; Charleston County, South Carolina was the scene of one of the most bitter strikes in recent history, as will be described shortly.

Public interest in employee organization is usually limited until contract bargaining becomes intense or a seemingly small incident ignites a strike. Sometimes voters are deliberately kept in the dark because of delicate negotiations. The public has a tendency to favor quick concessions to the workers to end strikes, though, just as with any controversy, the issues become confused and change as the dispute gains momentum. The hospital workers' strike in Charleston County, South Carolina is an example.[18]

On March 28, 1969, 100 nonprofessional employees of the Charleston County Hospital did not show up for work. According to the county manager, the county had not had a history of bad relations with employees and the strike caught the county commissioners by complete surprise. The strike was underway for several hours before the workers and the commissioners got together to decide what the issues were. According to the county manager, the strike was called in sympathy for 300 nonprofessionals who were striking Charleston's State University Medical Hospital to protest dismissal of twelve employees and "to force union recognition on the state of South Carolina." In his view,

"... the 113-day strike... (at the Charleston County Hospital) and at the state medical university hospital was not necessarily the result of local grievances. During the most crucial periods of the strikes, workers' complaints appeared to be overshadowed if not lost in the excitement and emotionalism caused by a variety of outside influences, including particularly the national news media. The strikes attracted nationally prominent

112

political, governmental, labor union, and civil rights figures. They also attracted militants and extremists of many ilks. . . from practically every part of the country. During the strike period demonstrations, confrontations, economic boycotts, injunctions, protests, threats, curfew, vandalism and arson occurred in the Charleston community. . . (t)he strikes originally had the full encouragement and support of influential labor union leaders from the AFL-CIO, Teamsters, and the United Auto Workers, the national presidents of AFL-CIO and the UAW made competitive contributions to the cause of the hospital strikers, and at one point the International Longshoremen's Association threatened to close the port of Charleston unless the strike was settled in the workers' favor."

Three days after the strike began, the Southern Christian Leadership Conference publicly announced its support, and Mr. Ralph David Abernathy and Mrs. Martin Luther King Jr. came to Charleston. Even the White House became involved in arranging a settlement of the historic strike. As the county manager put it, "What had originally been considered a labor dispute case became a labor dispute cause with the introduction of modus operandi and techniques conditioned to the streets and not to the conference table." Of course, there were civil rights and racial overtones; the original twelve dismissed employees were black women, as well as all of the strikers.

Strikes can be precipitated by relatively minor incidents involving the union or its leadership, the government, or differences between rival unions. In Cleveland in August 1969, a two-week strike resulted when a local union steward stopped a city truck from entering a water and sewer maintenance yard.[19] The steward was suspended and threatened with discharge by the city. The union objected, demanded his reinstatement and when the city would not go along, the strike was on.

It all began when a water truck was converted to a supply truck, which led to a claim by the steward of Local 100 of the American Federation of State, County and Municipal Employees (AFSCME) that the city was breaking its agreement with the union by changing the function of the truck and having a member of the teamsters' union drive it. The AFSCME steward claimed that because the truck actually was a water truck it should have been driven by an AFSCME member. The steward further claimed that Cleveland officials had changed a job classification without notifying the local. The city countered that it had tried unsuccessfully to contact Local 100 leaders about the change. An agreement regarding the truck driver incident was almost settled by allowing a teamster to drive if accompanied by a Local 100 member as a helper, but, somehow, communication bogged down and city officials who had not been present during the compromise agreement telephoned to notify the steward he was suspended.

As the strike progressed other grievances surfaced and other factors assumed immense importance. The fiery steward of Local 100 maintained the city utilities director was pursuing a "personal vendetta" against him. Cleveland officials said Local 100 frequently violated civil service rules and regulations and had engineered wildcat strikes. Rival unions had little sympathy for the strikers, who in their view belonged to a local that had raided their unions for new members. Indeed, in 1969 Local 100 membership totaled about 1300 water service and sewer maintenance employees, airport safety workers and some personnel from other city departments, compared to a 1965 membership of only 450.

Racial factors played an important part in the dispute. Local 100 consists primarily of black workers. Cleveland's mayor was also black, his reelection was fast approaching and he needed labor's support to win. Labor, including the 14 public employee unions, had supported the mayor's first election and generally had had a fine relationship with city hall — with the exception of occasional problems with Local 100's steward. As the strike wore on and both sides became more in-

114

transigent, the national AFSCME president, who was white, became alarmed that the local might try to mobilize the entire black community to vote against the mayor in the upcoming election. AFSCME did not want to be in the "position of the white leadership of this union being responsible for the defeat of a black mayor." Consequently, the national office was instrumental in finding an outside mediator to settle the dispute.

Meanwhile, the city and the union were at loggerheads over whether to suspend the steward or fire him. Suspension seemed a possibility until the president of Local 100 appeared on television demanding the resignation of the utilities director and the union soon followed by sending some members to the utilities department headquarters where they allegedly forced some clerical personnel to leave the building and join the strikers.

Cleveland's mayor also made a television appearance. In his view, the issue was not what to do with the militant steward, but "whether a union has the right to accomplish its objectives, no matter how unreasonable, or arbitrary, by resorting to illegal wildcat strike actions and other illegal pressures. . . . (T)he city has no choice but to be firm and insist that the contract procedures be followed. If we fail in this dispute, then our 1968 negotiations are worthless and we might as well throw away all our labor contracts." The issue was finally settled with the help of the outside mediator and a top secret meeting between the mayor and the AFSCME national president.

In union disputes the facts may never be clear. Many times the general public may be the innocent victim, but its sentiments influence and usually hasten a settlement. Both government leaders and strikers know the public becomes irate at the inconvenience of breakdowns in services, but they also believe citizens make independent judgments of who is right and who is wrong, tending to support increases for underpaid workers and other worthy causes while showing little tolerance for disruptions due to minor infringements of contracts. Both sides vie for public support, knowing that citizen backing is a powerful asset to bring to the negotiating table.

Who Joins What

Public employees holding almost any kind of job join unions or professional associations. They join industrial type unions, craft unions devoted to the interests of particular occupations, and professional associations. Some of these organizations are affiliated with the AFL-CIO and other national groups, others are independent; nationally some are composed only of people working for governments, while others enroll both public and private employees. Unlike the private sector, where unionism is confined to workers, unionism among public officials spills over to professionals, especially schoolteachers, and to what could be considered management. New York State's Taylor Law covering labor-management relations originally gave all county employees, including county managers and department heads the right to be organized and represented. Thus, when Rockland County negotiated its first contract under the Taylor Law with the local Civil Service Employees Association (CSEA), all labor and management members of the organization were covered except department heads and their deputies. Rockland County officials soon found it untenable to have management on both sides of the negotiating table, and when the Taylor Law was amended, the officials acted to remove management positions from contract coverage.[20]

Generally, public workers join one of seven unions. The few counties which handle public schools may deal with two additional teachers' organizations, the National Education Association and the American Federation of Teachers. Each is different in outlook and style of working with local governments.[21]

116

—*American Federation of State, County and Municipal Employees (AFSCME)* is a union on the move. At least 500,000 employees are members and its president, Jerry Wurf, claims that 1000 people join each week. Persons employed at all kinds of jobs — from zoo keeper to architect — belong, and it is organized primarily on an industrial rather than a craft basis. In the 1930s, when it originated, AFSCME had a white collar image but now blue collar workers are included (such as the water service and sewer maintenance workers in Cleveland and highway maintenance employees in Rockland County, New York). It was during the AFSCME campaign to organize garbage collectors in Memphis that Dr. Martin Luther King, Jr. was assassinated. There are more than 2400 local unions, primarily in New England and the Northeast, which have more than 1000 agreements with cities and counties.

—*International Association of Fire Fighters (IAFF)* is one of the oldest public employee unions, established more than 50 years ago. It is the only public employee union adhering closely to the craft concept of organization. The IAFF was formed as a fraternal and social group but soon assumed the trappings of a union. Its members are permanent employees engaged in fire fighting, fire communications and prevention; everyone can belong, right up to the fire chief, battalion chiefs and other officers. The IAFF claims to have organized about 85 percent of its potential membership. By 1972 the organization had expanded to about 1700 locals, but some of these are small, with a dozen or so members. The IAFF campaigns for more pay, a standard 40 hour work week, better training and uniform manning schedules.

—Policemen belong to several organizations but the largest is the *Fraternal Order of Police (FOP)*. The FOP has members in about 45 percent of all cities with

117

organized employees. It does not consider itself a union but many of its 300 or so local lodges take part in bargaining, handle grievances and represent other police interests. The overriding concern of the FOP is to increase pensions and improve working conditions.

One of the most visible groups seeking better pay for policemen is the *Patrolman's Benevolent Association (PBA)* in New York City. The former leader of that group is now trying to form a national police union known as the *International Brotherhood of Police Officers* as a subsidiary of the *Service Employees International Union (SEIU)*. The SEIU now claims about 6000 police members, mainly in medium sized cities, but establishing a national union may be difficult since many policemen seem content with the FOP or the local police associations that exist in 41 percent of cities where employees have organized.

—*Service Employees International Union (SEIU)*. This union, originally known as the Building Service Employees International, differs from the others which have been mentioned because it includes both public and private workers. The bulk of its members maintain, clean, service and operate private buildings, but about 35 percent of its 500,000 members work for government. The SEIU publicly employed members are drawn from several professional, blue-collar and uniformed occupations. Social workers, janitors, court clerks, and practical nurses belong, and as was mentioned, attempts are being made to enlist more policemen.

SEIU recently began a major campaign to double its membership by the mid-1970s. In the president's words, "We have to grow in size to the point where people in high places, like members of Congress and state legislatures, national employers and associations of administrators, will know there is a strong and powerful Service Employees Union." The organization has made

118

a special effort in California to work with employee associations, perhaps with an eye toward eventual merger.

—*Laborers' International Union (LIU).* Like the Service Employees International, the LIU has members who work for both private and public employers. About 90,000 of its 600,000 members work for government, usually in public works, sewer and water departments; about two-thirds are in blue-collar work and the rest are white collar workers or in the social services. LIU locals are found mainly in medium sized cities without a history of union activity. It is one of the few AFL-CIO affiliates that has made headway in organizing minorities, and the union estimates that about 40 percent of its total members are black, Mexican-Americans or Puerto Ricans. In the early 1970s, the union scored a breakthrough in organizing workers in Montgomery and Birmingham, Alabama, and it is making inroads in other southern states, especially Florida, Arkansas, Texas, Tennessee and Georgia.

—*International Brotherhood of Teamsters.* The Teamsters have about two million members, and close to 100,000 of them work for governments. Most of its public employee members work for turnpikes and state colleges, but they also include municipal and county employees, as was mentioned in the Cleveland labor dispute described earlier. Despite the adverse publicity the Teamsters received from the Senate racketeering hearings and the imprisonment of Jimmy Hoffa, its membership has continued to expand, both public and private.

—The national unions — AFSCME, SEIU, LIU and Teamsters — are well known and strong, but they are not the only important public employee organizations. A considerable number of local and state associations, usually named employee association or civil service association, are also well entrenched and growing in importance, although they have received far less publicity.

There are close to 700 such organizations in various cities and counties, with a membership of about 270,000. Many of them are found in the west coast states — California, Washington, and Oregon — and to a lesser degree in the northeastern states. These organizations differ considerably from the traditional unions. They rely on traditional methods of lobbying and civil service procedures to press their demands for increased pay and better working conditions. In the words of John R. Doyle, president of a national coalition of local associations (AGE — see below), "The independent associations are extremely strong advocates of the merit system principle." Many unions look upon these groups as "company unions."

Some of the associations are changing their tactics, however. In California, the 110,000 member state employees association abandoned its no-strike pledge. The associations' support for traditional civil service procedures should not obscure their strength and their following among public employees. They have emerged as formidable opponents to the AFL-CIO in New York, California, Michigan, New Jersey and a few other states. The New York State Civil Service Employees Association recently dropped its no-strike pledge to win the continued representation of 170,000 state workers over a challenge by AFSCME. In order to gain nationwide attention and increase their political strength, many of the independent local associations formed a coalition, the *Assembly of Governmental Employees* (AGE). In 1969 the coalition claimed a total membership of 500,000, equal to the AFSCME. The first purpose of the group is to extend and uphold the civil service merit system. (AGE) "believes the selection and promotion of public employees should be based upon demonstrated merit as determined by competitive examination," but like unions, the local members' organizations engage in collective bargaining.

Why Organize? The Seeds for
Labor-Management Disputes

For years the public bureaucracy was considered one of the most stable and conservative forces in the American political system — politicians came and went but the bureaucrats stayed on. Salaries were low, it was conceded, but the meager pay was supposed to be compensated for by job security, paid vacations and ample sick leave.

Public employees are no longer so secure, with RIFs (reductions in force) occurring more frequently and taxpayers becoming restive about local government expenditures. (Although taxpayers seem unwilling to foot the bill, they are not hesitant to demand more and better services.) As a result the public employee feels overworked and underpaid and to improve his condition joins with his colleagues to form a union. Increased wages and fringe benefits are his foremost objectives. "Complaints over wages and benefits have led to more man-day strike losses than any other single cause in the last dozen years"...U.S. Bureau of Labor Statistics. Losses in working time from these grievances are more than double the losses due to other major causes of strikes (union organization, job security, inter- or intra-union matters, working conditions, safety, and job assignments). In the last 15 years more than 2.5 million work days were lost because of wage disputes, compared to 2.2 million days for all other causes.[22]

The wage issue is complicated by the involvement of three parties to any dispute, the elected and administrative employers, the general public, and the employees and their union. In a sense all three groups are trapped by the issues. County commissioners and executives are caught between workers who demand pay and fringe benefits at least equal to the private sector, and the voters who clearly want the lid kept on spending. On the other hand, the employees may have a good case. Some laundry, food service and custodial workers have been poorly compensated everywhere for years. Some professionals are also underpaid. For example, teachers in Montgomery County, Maryland cannot afford a house in the county, and rental units in their price range are limited. The energy crisis promises to make their commuting problems even more burdensome. This is not unique to Montgomery County or to schoolteachers. Policemen and firemen face similar problems, not to mention garbage collectors and sanitation workers. At the same time public employees realize that better pay means higher taxes, in effect, taking money from one hand and putting it into another.

Sometimes a strike helps clear the air. In 1970 masses of San Francisco employees walked off their jobs. The strike, lasting only four days, was brought on by rank and file workers pressuring for large pay increases, countered by political leaders being pressured by citizens and community groups to hold the line on spending.[23] Accommodation was reached quickly, partly because both the workers and the government's leaders could understand the pressures faced by the other side. San Francisco had had a history of good relations between management and labor, both in government and in the private sector. Even in 1970, the year of the strike, the city and its rank and file employees were on good terms. Part of this friendship and mutual respect was due to San Francisco's mayor who had been involved in labor-management relations before taking office and who was elected with the backing of labor. But this relationship did not divert the strike.

Tensions began to mount during the city's budget preparation. Following the usual practice, the civil service commission forwarded to the board of supervisors a pay package for nearly 15,000 "miscellaneous" workers, a category including most employees except policemen, firemen, teachers, municipal railway drivers and craft union members covered under separate agreements. The budget

122

called for salary increases of about $9.5 million or a 7.5 percent increase.

The mayor and the board of supervisors were immediately hostile. The mayor announced that he would veto the entire proposal; the board of supervisors planned to reduce the increase to about 5 percent, the greatest cut in a civil service proposal in years. The mayor and the supervisors were extremely sensitive to San Francisco's recent "taxpayers' revolt." In the previous election, three bond issues had been defeated by a sizable margin, and two supervisors had lost reelection over a spending issue. In addition, when the civil service commission proposal was made public, city hall was flooded with mail overwhelmingly for a hard line against the pay increase. During discussions with the six employee organizations, the mayor and the supervisors refused to yield. In the words of the mayor— "You can't get blood out of a turnip, the property taxpayer has had it." Negotiations finally bogged down and the strike began March 13, 1970.

As other employee unions joined the strike, the city was effectively closed down. No schools, no buses, streetcars or cable cars operated. Hospital workers observed the picket lines. The streets were not swept. Both the mayor and the union leader quickly assembled a negotiating team. Both sides were anxious to limit the strike, not only because the city was near chaos, but because union members feared that a prolonged strike would be politically damaging to the mayor, a man they trusted and liked despite the disagreement. As negotiations progressed and it became apparent that labor and management agreed on basics — that a pay increase was due and that both sides needed to save face with the general public — the major issue became how to give workers an increase without seeming to defy the taxpayer revolt. A major breakthrough came when two representatives of the employees discovered that the civil service commission had overestimated the pay increase by about $1 million, which gave the mayor room for a compromise with the board of supervisors and the public. On the other side, unions representing other city employees, having already settled their pay increases, pressured the striking unions to accept a compromise and get on with taking care of the city. A compromise acceptable to everyone was reached quickly.

Money is not the only basis for labor-management disagreements. Psychological factors, although not always easy to define, also play a role. Often in large bureaucracies the individual feels he cannot be heard, that he merely occupies a position in the job classification and pay scale. Management does not really regard him as an individual. Members of minority groups, such as in Charleston County, South Carolina feel they have been underpaid and deprived of opportunities for years. Minority workers' grievances constitute a major new element in labor relations in the last 15 years, as complaints about discrimination of various sorts have been made. Most of the complaints allege that the employer was biased in making promotions or job assignments.

In the past, many of these issues were handled by independent civil service commissions, but as the years have gone by, these commissions appear to have become the spokesmen for management, enacting personnel policies rather than assuring that the voice of the employees is heard. This does not apply to all civil service commissions. In many cities and counties civil service associations are the major competitors of unions for new members. Generally, many feel that civil service is a thing of the past, although these commissions still handle formal grievance procedures, and a limited number have taken part in labor-management negotiations.

Disputes can arise over a variety of other issues. There are union demands for official recognition of the representatives of employees, and union demands that employees have a voice in determining working conditions, especially case loads and classroom sizes, sometimes even curriculum. Disputes over working conditions can spill over quickly into

124

policy matters. The county official facing a demand for smaller classes from the local chapter of the National Education Association finds that the association is directly affecting his right to determine budgets and capital programming. He can trim classroom sizes by hiring more teachers, which will drive the budget up. This also may require more classrooms, which means construction and a possible bond referendum.

The Effect of Unions on Local Government

Whether the explosion of public unionism has been good or bad, it has caused substantive changes in government services, finances, personnel policies and numerous administrative procedures. Because public unions are a relatively recent phenomenon, many executives and governing board members are unfamiliar with labor relations and the techniques of negotiating with unions and professional associations. They have had to catch up quickly, and at times personnel matters have been shoved to a number one priority from their former low place on the list, if they were on the list at all.

Rockland County, near New York City, was one of those counties surprised by the Taylor Law of 1967. Suddenly county officials were required to meet with organizations representing public employees and to enter collective bargaining negotiations culminating in a signed contract. According to the county personnel officer, no one in the Rockland County government was prepared for the new law. "None of us at the county level had any experience in labor relations. And this was generally true throughout the state of New York."[24] Rockland officials, as their counterparts in many counties were forced to, let other matters slide while devoting full time to becoming informed. Some counties hired consultants with private labor-management experience; others sent personnel staff members and civil service commission personnel to special schools and seminars. Rockland officials held seminars, inviting officials from nearby counties. They sought advice from the Cornell University School of Industrial and Labor Relations. They asked state officials to explain exactly what the Taylor Law meant and what the county was required to do. They learned the terminology—unit determination, collective bargaining, fact finding, meet and confer, and so forth. After one full year of intensive study, the county took steps to recognize employee representatives formally and to begin negotiations.

Many county officials also have been in a quandary because of the attitudes of their state. Historically the Statehouse was specific about what counties could and could not do, but many were silent about how to react to the organization of employees. For many years state legislatures willingly let the courts and the bureaucracy settle labor problems. Because states so often had strait-jacketed them, local officials were reticent to chart an independent course on such a controversial issue. In the absence of guidelines some counties engaged in de facto bargaining while others refused to negotiate, claiming that they lacked state authorization to do so. On the other hand, some states flatly denied permission for the counties to bargain. Regardless of the situation, employees joined unions, in some cases even walked off their jobs. The counties had to end the strikes somehow.

The Charleston County strike described earlier is a good example. From the start it was recognized throughout the state that public employees had the constitutional right to join a union. But the state constitution prohibited local officials from entering into collective bargaining contracts, memoranda of understanding or any other legal agreement with a labor group. In effect the local official could not recognize the union as the bargaining representative of the employees. As the county manager put it,

Employment policies negotiated and signed by representatives of public agencies constitute either an illegal delegation of legislative power or an illegal usurpation of legislative power on the part of the public agencies represented. Accordingly, a contract or agreement arrived at by collective bargaining is illegal and unenforceable.[25]

Nevertheless, the hospital employees went on strike, and the county had to deal with the union, or at least its leadership, if it was to get anywhere. County officials decided to communicate with the workers (not the union) through community organizations which were in a position to know the workers and their grievances, such as the ministerial association and neighborhood groups. Eventually, county officials negotiated directly with five workers, again not union leaders, who represented the group.

Recently, state legislatures have asserted more leadership, now that they have contended with the union movement among their own employees. Wisconsin pioneered in 1959 by enacting a comprehensive law. In 1967 alone, 17 states passed new laws covering some aspect of labor-management affairs. By 1972, 21 states had general statutes requiring public employers to engage in collective negotiations or to "meet and confer" with certain employee representatives. Other states authorized counties and cities to meet, confer or enter collective bargaining if they wished, or merely to outline basic organizational rights for public personnel. County officials must negotiate with employee representatives in Delaware, Hawaii, Massachusetts, New Jersey, New York, Oregon, Pennsylvania, Washington, Wisconsin, Michigan and Nevada. County officials in California are required to "meet and confer with union officials in good faith." Similar requirements exist in Minnesota, Missouri and South Dakota. More than 25 states have specified occupational categories for collective bargaining and meet and confer laws, usually teachers, firemen, policemen, public utility and transportation employees, nurses, hospital workers and university personnel, because of their political strength or the uniqueness or essentiality of their functions.[26] Each state has a different approach to the rights of employees and the obligations of employers; all agree, however, on the right of public employees to organize, on the obligation of cities and counties to conduct hearings on charges of unfair practices, and on the responsibility of both employer and employee to use mediation and fact-finding to resolve impasses.

One of the most noticeable results of public unions has been the extent to which services have been disrupted by strikes. During the first half of 1970, a city or county was hit by a walkout every three days.[27] If the dispute did not result in a strike, there were work slowdowns or employees staying home "sick." In 1958 there were only fifteen strikes involving less than 2000 state and local workers. By 1968 there were 254 strikes by 200,000 workers, and by 1969 the number of strikes had risen to over 400, though the number of employees involved remained about the same. The statistics for 1970 are similar, indicating that the problem may be leveling off; though, during the first 80 days of 1971, there were 50 strikes for local eastern employees alone (excluding teachers), compared to only 24 for the same period of 1970.[28] The number of strikes and man-hours off the job seems irrelevant compared to the mounting piles of garbage and trash on the curbs, the days of learning lost or the threats to public safety from reduced police protection. At the least, disruption of services is inconvenient; at the worst it can pose serious health and security problems. Usually, major chaos is avoided by settlements, and the former strikers collect the garbage, clean the streets and work long hours to put the county or city back in normal working condition — and collect overtime pay for their efforts.

Unions have been successful in seeking higher wages for their memberships, with great impact on the budgets and finances of local governments. As one expert put it,

Although it is thunderously proclaimed that management alone determines the budget, later it is quietly announced that the number of new positions requested for a particular department has been substantially increased. Management both decided — and listened to the unions.[28]

Personnel costs are about 70 percent of all county budgets, and the percentage is increasing. Of course, not all the increase is due to employee organizations; some is due to inflation, some to expansion of public services, and some to higher quality service which requires a more specialized, competent staff. However, it has been estimated that if a union encompassing most of the city or county employees wins a 7 percent increase in pay and benefits, the operating budget may be increased by about 4 percent, even if nothing else goes up.[30] To cover this cost — because most states require their cities and counties to pass a balanced budget — the government must increase taxes — on property, earnings, sales, etc. Sometimes unions try to help county officials figure out where to get the money. Fact-finding panels in Detroit in 1968 and in Portland, Oregon in 1970 judged the appropriateness and level of the city revenue measures, and an article appearing recently in the *Industrial and Labor Relations Review* suggested ways labor arbitrators could determine the community's ability to pay.[31] The higher costs have stimulated greater public interest in government employees with new pressures for assessment and evaluation of the productivity and effectiveness of the work force.

Many cities and counties have budgeting schedules which do not mesh with bargaining schedules. Ideally, the unions and management should agree before the budget is submitted for official approval, but often this does not happen. As a result, labor probes management's resolve and apparent capacity to pay, and management usually keeps funds in reserve to cover increased employee wages. If the funds are identified by alert union representatives, however, they may use them as a floor for demands. If they are "hidden" in the budget or spread among various programs, public officials are tampering with the integrity of the budgeting process. If bargaining is lengthy, the county may have no choice but to pass a budget before settlement is reached, with the hope of finding money to meet the demands later on. In 1969 the city of St. Louis could not balance its budget which included a substantial pay increase negotiated with unions, until the state legislature had authorized a one percent increase in the sales tax. Balancing the budget is an inherently difficult task in any county, and the demands of employees' organizations and unions complicate the process.

The fight for higher pay has not been the only impact of unions. In the words of former Mayor John Lindsay:

> Labor militance has also created special problems for government. . . . Teachers now want to bargain about more than salaries. They also want to bargain about class size, about the curriculum. Social workers want to talk about the level of benefits for welfare recipients. Police want their say about the number of men on patrol and the authority to make arrests. Interns want to influence the quality of medical services and nurses are concerned with the number of duty stations.[32]

Unions are making headway in influencing decisions formerly regarded as the prerogative of management only. In Dade County, Florida for example, the county manager, after bargaining with firemen, agreed to recommend a specified number of men to work with different types of equipment. At various times, New York City patrolmen have insisted that they work in pairs for safety reasons. Marin County, California social workers' Local 535 has requested staffing changes in the welfare department.[33]

Labor unions have also had an impact on the distribution of work assignments. The result...less flexibility in deploying personnel at a time when governments must make the best use of each employee. As a result of negotiations, New Castle County, Delaware officials agreed not to assign employees to overtime work without their consent. The Cleveland strike described earlier was prompted by the city's decision to use a truck for more than one type of job. Unions are also determined to ensure that work is assigned according to specifications, that firemen are fighting fires, not repairing hydrants, that policemen are apprehending offenders, not operating tow trucks, and so on. If a policeman does perform other kinds of work, usually only with union consent, he must be paid for doing something out of the ordinary.

While such actions are to protect employees, a continuation of the trend could put local governments in the same "featherbedding" situation faced by the railroads and other industries where the labor needs have changed, but where the unions have forced retention of unnecessary personnel in unnecessary jobs.

Unions also are affecting personnel systems. For the few local governments which continue to hand out jobs as political favors, unions are forcing an adoption of merit principles and the hiring of qualified people. Where the cities and counties are already operating under the merit system and/or with civil service commissions, on the other hand, unions are charging that the programs are simply tools of management. The union alternative, in many cases, is no more flexible or forward looking than the present system. For example, they are unreceptive to a reduction of height requirements for policemen or the elimination of a college degree as a qualification for a caseworker.[34] However, unions have made few demands or complaints about government recruiting or hiring methods. Instead, their target has been promotions, with some success. Many of their requests are status quo oriented. They favor seniority, among the qualified, as the main criterion for advancement. They favor use of promotion lists instead of open competitive lists, and of promotions within a department instead of government-wide considerations. Of course, where grievances are involved, unions want management — not an independent civil service commission — to deal with them, and there has been a noticeable trend toward union negotiation of employee complaints about supervisors. Other grievances, suspension, demotion, or firing, are usually handled by civil service commissions where they exist. However, this also may change.

Unions have become increasingly aggressive in local, state and national politics. As one observer said,

> They are formidable political blocs, commanding enough votes to swing some municipal elections and wielding enough lobbying strength to shake many city councils. Above all, they have the power to shut down the governments... An executive clothed in the armor of an antistrike law is as fully clad as the emperor in the fable.[35]

Unions are flexing political muscle in state houses and in the United States Congress as well as in city halls and county courthouses. AFSCME president Jerry Wurf recently formed a coalition of all public employee unions to make greater impact on state legislatures and Congress, and to bolster the organizations' lobbying ability. AFSCME is also supporting a federal law to impose a collective bargaining system on all states.

Wurf's main ambition is to influence the federal government.[36] AFSCME endorsed Senator Edmund Muskie for the Democratic presidential nomination in 1972 before he withdrew, and worked hard for selected congressional candidates. The Service Employees International Union (SEIU) is making an all-out effort to double its membership among both public and private employees by 1976. According to the president: "When we have a million members we'll really have the clout we need to win the recognition, wages, and conditions our members deserve."[37]

132

Americans have virtually abandoned the notion that change is synonymous with progress and that progress is good. There is a growing realization that one change sets in motion a series of other changes — intended and unexpected, desirable and undesirable. Public employee organizations have changed personnel systems, management practices, budgets and attitudes. On the one hand the union movement has prompted more responsive and effective public programs, but in some ways they are "bureaucratizing" a system already notorious for its rigidity.

Some changes have involved government principles which should have been updated long ago. The idea that city and county officials should set pay and working conditions unilaterally as part of the exercise of their sovereign powers has given way to bilateral negotiations. An arbitrary and paternalistic system has been modified to reflect employee rights comparable to those in the private sector. It is no longer felt that an employee should relinquish those rights if he chooses government employment.

On the other hand contract issues can easily cross the border between working conditions and public policy. As union members public employees are members of the general public lobbying for what they want. There is no reason why public employees, as a special interest, should have the "inner track" on decisions which affect the entire community. Most of these decisions ultimately affect county budgets and the taxpayers' pocketbooks. To date taxpayers have not reacted directly to union developments, voicing their concerns, rather, about the increased costs of the government in general.

The aggressiveness of employee organizations has forced public officials to hide budget funds which can be later used to meet wage and salary demands. In addition contract negotiations are sometimes extremely secretive. According to one administrator, "Too often the final package is announced by management and union representatives after a long

133

'blackout' period during which the press and the public are told very little..."[38]

Not infrequently unions have been sensitive to the fiscal crunch experienced by their employers. At the same time, the accelerating costs of local government have heightened the interest of citizens and their public officials in measuring the productivity of their employees, a tricky undertaking for service-oriented jobs. Often for the first time in history, local governments are evaluating their programs in order to spot inefficiencies and waste.

The employees are shaking up the merit principles and civil service systems, but it is not yet clear that their alternatives would be superior to what exists. Some view unions and collective bargaining as "an excellent antidote for the evils of bureaucracy" by making individual employees feel that their voice is being heard. It also has been said that the unions define merit as an employee's ability to perform duties as measured by seniority, not competence.

In an age of tight budgets and complex local problems, flexible and aggressive governments are essential. Public unions have raised the spectre of increased costs and restrictive work rules at the same time that they have brought about a streamlined and more contemporary approach to public personnel systems. The political scientist Felix Nigro sums it up this way:

> There is no inexorable force which will make collective bargaining turn out one way or another, nor are the developments so swift as to make it problematic that humans can shape the future picture. Dramatic as unionism is, its significance has not yet been appreciated by enough of the public or, for that matter, of public management.[38]

Notes

1. Abernethy, Bob and Art White, "The Invisible Growth Machine," *Los Angeles Times West Magazine,* May 28, 1972.

2. *From America's Counties Today,* (Washington, D.C.: National Association of Counties, 1973), p. 39.

3. Stanley, David T., *Managing Local Government Under Union Pressure* (Washington, D.C.: The Brookings Institution, 1972), p. 120.

4. Miller, Glenn W., "Manpower in the Public Sector," *Public Personnel Management,* vol. XXXII no. 1, January 1972, p. 50.

5. *Ibid.*

6. For discussions of the accountability of public servants to citizens, see Charles D. Adrian, *State and Local Governments,* 3rd ed., (New York: McGraw-Hill Book Company, 1972), p. 305-306 and Frederick Mosher, *Democracy and the Public Service.* (New York: Oxford University Press, 1968).

7. Stenberg, Carl, *"Labor-Management Relations in State and Local Government: Progress and Prospects,"- Public Administration Review,* vol. XXXII, no. 2, March/ April 1972, p. 102.

8. *Ibid.,* and Eaton, William J., "A Look at Public Employee Unions," (Washington, D.C.: Labor-Management Relations Service, July 1972, p. 4.

9. Stenberg, *op. cit.*

10. Zagoria, Sam, "National Overview of County Labor Relations," Remarks before workshop held during the 36th Annual Conference of the National Association of Counties, Milwaukee, Wisconsin, July 1971.

11. Nigro, Felix A., "The Implications for Public Administration," *Public Administration Review,* vol. XXXII, no. 2, March/April 1972, p. 120.

12. Henry, David B. and James J. Banner, in "Labor-Management Relations in Two Counties," *The American County,* March 1970, p. 36.

13. *Ibid.*

14. Webb, Walter, "Government Manpower: An Overview," *Municipal Yearbook, 1971,* (Washington, D.C.: International City Management Association), p. 173-197.

15. Rosen, Harold S., "An Alternative: Meet and Confer — The Experience in Santa Clara County, California," (Washington, D.C.: Labor-Management Relations Service, November 1972), p. 7.

16. Webb, *op. cit.*

17. Black, Richard, "The Charleston County Experience," Remarks before workshop held during the 36th Annual Conference of the National Association of Counties, Milwaukee, Wisconsin, July 1971.

18. *Ibid.*

19. Grimes, John A., "Work Stoppages: A Tale of Three Cities," (Washington, D.C.: Labor-Management Relations Service, May 1970), p. 3-6.

20. Anderson, James K., "The Rockland County Experience," Remarks before workshop held during the 36th Annual Conference of the National Association of Counties, Milwaukee, Wisconsin, July 1971.

21. Based on information obtained from Eaton, *op. cit.*

22. Sharkey, Samuel M., Jr., "Public Employee Strikes: Causes and Effects," (Washington, D.C.: Labor-Management Relations Service, December 1970), p. 5.

23. Grimes, *op. cit.*

24. Anderson, *op. cit.*

25. Black, *op. cit.*

26. Stenberg, *op. cit.*

27. Sharkey, *op. cit.*

28. Stenberg, *op. cit.*

29. Nigro, *op. cit.*

30. Stanley, David T., "Change: The Impact of Unions

on Local Government," (Washington, D.C.: Labor-Management Relations Service, March 1971), p. 4.

31. *Ibid.*
32. Black, *op. cit.*
33. Stanley, *op. cit.*
34. *Ibid.*, p. 2.
35. *Ibid.*, p. 1.
36. Eaton, *op. cit.*
37. *Ibid.*
38. Nigro, *op. cit.*

6.   The Struggle for Regional Cooperation

The Need for Joint Action

Despite the heat and stale smoggy air of August 1973, history was made. The Los Angeles mayor and city officials sat down with the five county supervisors to discuss issues of mutual concern and how the city and county could cooperate to deal with them. A major accomplishment? Perhaps not, but there hadn't been such a meeting for at least twenty years, despite three million common constituents, some jointly administered programs, and mutual assistance in financing new hospitals and other major facilities. The city and county officials may try to ignore each other, but their governments are too geographically, socially and functionally integrated.[1]

With few exceptions every county, large or small, urban or rural, encompasses cities and towns. A large percentage of America's 190 million county residents also lives in cities. Considering the 30,000 city and town jurisdictions within counties which have their own governing responsibilities, it is inevitable that paths should cross, with both mutual frustration and cooperation.

Too often the governments in a locality are at each other's throats, such as Los Angeles, where the city fights the county and both in turn fight the suburban municipalities. The stakes are economic and social. All local governments, especially urban ones must offer more services at a better quality to a rapidly growing population. Concurrently they must replace obsolete equipment and repair or replace dilapidated buildings. The costs are high, and taxes, especially on property, are the major source of funds. Local governments must compete among themselves for the available income and property on which to levy taxes. Unlike commercial corporations, they cannot declare bankruptcy (although a few did during the depression); they must struggle on.

Local government conflicts also exist because of differences among their constituents in social status, life styles, education, wealth, ethnic groupings, etc. While any one government houses a mixture of citizens, each seems to have its own personality. Originally county and city boundaries were drawn to facilitate public services and the operations of government. County boundaries were defined arbitrarily, but cities were developed to serve clusters of residents. Through the years however, many governments, especially in the suburbs, were created more for social and political reasons than for functional ones, more to keep others out and preserve small government than to perform operations essential to a community. Many of these units are too small to provide services efficiently, but their residents resist combinations with larger governments in order to "protect their lifestyles."

Conflicting social attitudes and competition over a tax base explain the fight between Milwaukee and the 18 suburbs of Milwaukee County.[2] In the early 1900s industry began to move from the city to cheaper suburban land. Feeling the economic pinch, Milwaukee officials repeatedly urged the combination of the city, suburbs and county into one areawide jurisdiction with a large tax base. The idea was always vetoed. Realizing that consolidation was dead, the Milwaukee mayor announced a major annexation campaign, setting up a department of annexation to follow through, with great success. Within ten years the city grew from 26 square miles to 44. Un-

140

der a different mayor, a second annexation campaign again doubled the size of the city by 1957.

Leaders of the other jurisdictions immediately fought back to prevent their own takeover by Milwaukee. Suburban mayors began annexation campaigns, and unincorporated areas began to incorporate. Suburbanites were fearful of losing their small community-oriented governments and a middle-upper middle class lifestyle. They were anxious to enlarge and strengthen their own tax bases as well.

With all the land now claimed by a city or town, the struggle to change political boundaries in the Milwaukee area has come to an end, but the city and its suburbs continue to fight. In 1968 the mayor directed his budget office to determine how much Milwaukee was spending to subsidize its suburbs. The finding was $12 to $14 million annually. Suburban officials countered that they provided jobs for central city residents, housed a county hospital used by everyone, and paid county taxes which were spent in Milwaukee. The arguing carried over to social issues. The mayor charged that suburban zoning regulations call for expensive housing just to keep out the poor and the blacks, which the local jurisdictions vigorously deny.

In the meantime an aggressive Milwaukee County government, headed by an elected executive and a council, has eased the financial and service burdens of the municipalities by assuming responsibility for various areawide functions, particularly parks, hospitals and health and welfare services. The county executive has tried to bring all the governments in the area together through the Intergovernmental Cooperation Council which, after five years of concerted effort, was formed in 1968. However, Milwaukee City refuses to join until the voting system is based on population instead of the present system which allows each government one vote.

In many localities cities and counties also disagree over public services. As the tax bases of many cities have dried up, some municipal services have been shifted to the counties.

Due to their large territorial base, counties increasingly are being called upon to address regional problems; expressways, sewage disposal, etc. Urban population shifts — and the resulting shifts in taxable resources — have created an upsurge in county activity and a corresponding growth in political strength. The typical central city is losing population to its suburbs and in many areas the county population outside the city far outnumbers that within it. Buffalo, New York has a population of 462,783, only 41 percent of the Erie County population; Pittsburgh contains 520,000 people, only 33 percent of the Allegheny County population.[3]

The outflow of people usually divides among several suburban jurisdictions, none with enough population to exert political leadership for the area the way the central city did in its heyday, having too many differences to take a united stand on many issues. Most of those leaving Buffalo, for example, move to one of eighteen municipalities; most of those leaving Pittsburgh move to one of eighty-five municipalities. County officials, as spokesmen for both city and suburb, often step into the breach to assume political power. This also can happen where the core city contains a substantial proportion of the county residents. Milwaukee houses 67 percent of the county population, but as one local observer noted, "Because of the urban spectres of population flight and blight and greater area diversity, the power to decide the more urgent policies has increasingly shifted from its hands to the suburban and county governments . . ."[4]

Neighboring governments do not always bicker. Despite their differences, constituents often are brought together by economic interdependencies, pride in the professional football team, the need to clean a polluted river, a drive on area drug abuse, or a host of other factors. In Minneapolis–St. Paul several issues have supplanted rivalries among two cities, 36 suburbs and six counties. There is the economic threat from other major population centers in the country. Mayors, county officials and citizens began to realize in economic growth, as in professional sports, the critical competition. . . is not (among) themselves but between the Twin Cities area as a whole and the other metropolitan complexes: Kansas City, San Francisco, Chicago, Atlanta.[5]

Another factor encouraging joint action by governments in the Minneapolis-St. Paul area was the consolidation of private institutions which had been organized previously according to the boundaries of local governments, such as trade associations, labor contracts, sales districts and numerous educational and cultural activities. Furthermore there were heavy investments by downtown corporations in outlying counties. Finally, the politicians recognized that slowly but steadily their service-providing powers were being undermined by special districts, each set up to furnish a single service throughout the region and all of them defiantly independent of efforts to coordinate their plans with those of cities and counties. Most of the special districts were governed by officials not directly accountable to local citizens or their elected officials, and many had ample tax authority. To bring some order to the growing chaos of fragmentation, the Minnesota legislature, with the blessing of local officials, created the Metropolitan Council in 1967. Its purpose was to oversee administration of services and facilities that were vital to overall regional development, such as the location of airports, construction of a sewage system, metropolitan transportation, etc. The council has brought focus and a movement toward concerted regional effort, where there had been a splintering of jurisdictions.

The struggle for regional cooperation is not exclusively urban. In northeastern Tennessee and adjacent Virginia, nine counties and twenty-two cities in the Appalachian Mountains formed the First Tennessee-Virginia Development District to make a joint attack on some crippling regional problems — poor roads, a poorly educated populace with a worrisome

143

dropout rate in the public schools, a glutted labor market exacerbated by the decline of farming, deficient health care, substandard housing, inadequate water and sewer facilities, poor fire protection, and on and on. The new district was not designed to operate programs; it was to be a vehicle for the discussion of problems by local officials with the objective of setting joint program priorities. Once the plans of action were set, the district assisted the local governments in their search for financing (particularly from the federal government), and it provided technical assistance in the implementation of programs.

This was a big change from the way it had been. In the words of one small-town mayor:

> For as long as I can remember, there was a division among the communities, even a great deal of hostile and unhealthy competition. Everybody stayed locked up within their own special jurisdiction, trying to take care of their own individual problems. Unsuccessfully I might add, in all too many cases. There was a void, and it was becoming obvious there was a need for regional cooperation as state and federal government relations with the communities were getting too complicated.[6]

Thanks to the First Tennessee–Virginia Development District, the nine-county area now boasts two regional industrial parks, new and expanded hospitals, and four new secondary vocational schools, among other achievements. As the Chairman of the Unicoi County, Tennessee, Court remarked, "Our small community of 15,000 just couldn't have done many of the things that have been accomplished without the district."[7]

Despite their many disagreements, municipal and county officials usually see eye to eye on the services their citizens need, and they are quick to realize when their own governments can't provide the quality demanded on an independent basis. At such times they readily look to each other for help.

144

Mutual assistance takes a variety of forms — from verbal assurances of aid during an emergency all the way to political reorganization. Joint action has traditionally centered around the necessity of financial cooperation, the pooling of resources to offer a service, but in recent years there has been a recognition that some services — transportation is one example — can be handled effectively only on a regional basis. Furthermore, discussion of the need to turn to areawide governments has centered on arguments of equity, the belief that all the region's citizens should have opportunities to participate in areawide decisions and that a government with a larger geographic base could distribute financial and social responsibilities more equitably. Whatever type of joint action is taken, it usually calls for an expanded role for counties.

Reassigning Service Responsibilities

City-county interaction most frequently focuses on which government will deliver specific services. Often the matter is settled by shifting responsibility from the city to the county, either at the request of the smaller government or the command of the state, or by a decision to furnish a service jointly. Large or small, rural or urban, cities contract extensively with counties for services. Rarely do counties buy services from municipalities. A comprehensive 1971 survey of over 2000 cities and 800 counties revealed 62 percent of the cities contracted with their counties for services. More than 70 percent of the densely populated counties (those having 500,000 or more residents) furnished services, but smaller counties were also called upon. The list of functions is varied... use of jails, police protection, road construction, welfare programs, park facilities, planning, and so on.[8] Usually, cities pick and choose what they want, entering a separate contract for each service.

Primarily cities use county services to save money and because some essential facilities, such as sewage treatment plants, are simply too costly for a small government to build and operate. Contracting is convenient and politically expedient: city-county contracts can be entered easily and terminated just as easily if they do not work out. Elected officials can, in most cases, set up the agreement without direct citizen approval, but if complaints are raised, the contract can be allowed to expire. Contracts are particularly attractive to the 1500 suburban communities with less than 1000 residents and their slightly larger neighbors, who are determined to preserve their small, "hometown" government with its independent control of zoning and land use, but lack a financial base to offer a full complement of urban services. The purchase of county support allows them the best of both political worlds.

For over one hundred years states have willingly permitted cities and counties to enter contracts and provide services jointly, an attitude which is surprising considering the usual restrictions they place on their subdivisions. An Indiana statute of 1852 authorized "any jail to be used to house a fugitive from justice," and entitled the jailer to "collect reasonable compensation from the officer having the prisoner in custody."[9] Today, all 50 states permit local governments to enter some type of service agreement or contract;[10] a few states regard the authority to work together as an inherent power of cities and counties and expect the governments on their own initiative to pass ordinances or resolutions to effect the cooperation. The majority of states, taking a more restrictive view of inherent local powers, have passed laws or constitutional provisions permitting service contracting and other types of cooperation. Some states pass one law giving blanket authorization for cooperation in any service the local government is authorized to provide; others enact separate laws affecting each function.

The following section of the New York constitution is typical of the former:

> Local governments shall have the power to agree, as authorized by act of the legislature, with the federal

government, a state or one or more other governments within or without the state, to provide cooperatively, jointly, or by contract any facilities, service, activity or undertaking which each participating local government has the power to provide separately.[11]

Minnesota has taken the service-by-service approach, which has resulted in approximately 110 laws allowing cooperation on specific services.[12] Most state laws are optional — cities and counties may choose to use them or ignore them. Texas is an exception. If cities in that state request a county to provide a service, the county is obligated to do so.[13] It should be emphasized that the authority to contract for services does not give counties the power to offer additional services; it simply empowers them to sell services they had the authority to offer anyway. The last phrase of the New York constitution cited earlier deserves another look: "Local governments [including counties] shall have the power. . . to provide . . . any facilities, service, activity or undertaking *which each participating local government has the power to provide separately.*"

Despite the fairly lenient attitude of most states, counties — even those in the same state — are timid about their authority to offer services to municipalities. County officials polled in six states (Alaska, California, Michigan, Montana, New York and Oregon) agreed that their governments could sell services to cities, but officials in 21 states were doubtful of their legal ability to do so, and in the remaining states, their opinions were divided.[14] Obviously, many county officials have not sought to increase their functional responsibilities as much as they could have.

The Lakewood Plan

Los Angeles County is an exception; the supervisors have been aggressive in using their full range of contracting powers. Though relations may have been strained between the county and the central city, the county has had ample interaction with suburban communities, especially since a unique service arrangement with Lakewood was established in 1954 whereby the city began buying all of its services from the county, except parks and recreation. All but two of the 32 Los Angeles suburbs incorporated since 1954 have followed suit. The county also sells numerous services to the 45 older communities (established before 1954), including Los Angeles, but not as extensively. Such comprehensive contracting has brought about a new era of city-county interdependence in the Los Angeles area.[15]

Several factors prompted the Lakewood arrangement, but the most immediate was the attempt by neighboring Long Beach to annex the smaller, more affluent suburb. Lakewood residents had no desire to become part of the older city and its social problems. They voted overwhelmingly against annexation when it was forced to a vote, but they knew their days as an unincorporated community were limited. An immediate exploration was begun to develop a defense against the takeover. At the same time, they had to avoid the expense of setting up a city government and the full array of employees, equipment and buildings necessary to provide the range and quality of services they were getting from the county. In California, once a community incorporates, urban services furnished by the county cease, and the city is expected to undertake its own programs.

During discussions with county officials, Lakewood representatives devised a plan: they would become a municipal government, but they would not provide public services. Instead, they would purchase what they needed from the county, becoming a "government without a bureaucracy." In terms of what citizens received, nothing would change, but they would have to pay the county a fee for services in addition to paying the regular county tax. The county agreed with the idea, and the Lakewood Plan was put into effect. A year later,

Lakewood received a financial uplift when the state legislature passed a local retail sales tax, giving the town a source of income in addition to the residential property tax. This law, plus the desire of citizens to control their own zoning, prompted other cities to incorporate in the same manner.

The Lakewood Plan was possible because the county had supplied municipal services since the early 1900s. As early as 1850, people in the Los Angeles area showed a preference for suburban or country living by a two to one margin, which required the county to get into the municipal services business. After adopting a home rule charter in 1912, the county developed such an array of services that only 45 communities felt the need to incorporate their own governments. The county took advantage of state laws to extend its municipal activities... it assumed functions formerly furnished by its cities after the authorization was granted by the California legislature in 1913; it set up special purpose districts to offer additional services following enactment of a state law in the 1920s; it offered services to cities through contracts as authorized by a statute enacted in the 1930s.

By 1950, the county offered all the urban services needed by the one million persons living in unincorporated communities either directly or through 266 special districts which it controlled. County departments were modern and professional, and supervised by a chief administrative officer. The fact that no new cities incorporated from 1939 to 1954 attests to the county's competence.

The Lakewood incorporation set off a chain reaction. Within a few years, 32 other cities followed suit, and they, like Lakewood, were "paper" cities, having a full complement of mayors and council members, but only one or two employees and no functional responsibilities. These suburbs had, as the county's chief administrative officer put it, "home rule plus economy — a city operation without large capital investments and fixed overhead, but retaining grass-roots government." They also had sophisticated public programs plus small town,

149

locally sensitive government and a protective wall between themselves and their neighbors.

Under the Lakewood Plan, cities decide which of the 60 county services they wish to buy, and contract for them. The "paper" cities contract for the basic necessities — police and fire protection, etc., plus any extras they want. Older cities also buy some county services, ranging from animal control to subdivision mapping. By 1970, Los Angeles County had entered about 1600 agreements with all 77 municipalities.

The services are paid for in a variety of ways. Animal regulation, for example, is covered by license fees; fire protection, libraries and a few others are financed by special taxing districts administered by the county. All other services are paid through direct reimbursements by residents of the contracting city, raised either through a property tax or payments from the state.

Although county-suburban relations are basically harmonious, friction occasionally results. One longstanding conflict is between the older municipalities (those formed before the Lakewood Plan) and the county; it centers on the equity of county taxes. Before the plan was developed, residents of older cities maintained that their county taxes were used to provide up-to-date urban services to citizens of unincorporated areas. The problem was that city residents paid a county tax plus a city tax for their municipal services; citizens in unincorporated communities paid a single county tax for both countywide and some municipal services. Other urban services were financed by county-controlled special taxing districts. The conflict reached its peak in the 1950s and has subsided somewhat because the county cut back on urban services and because many unincorporated sections became cities; but now the older cities direct the same financial argument to contract municipalities, claiming that contract cities do not pay for the full costs of the services they receive. Contract cities counter that indeed they do pay their way, and that non-contract cities could always choose to buy their services from the county. Two grand jury audits have shown that payments from all jurisdictions are equitable, but in some quarters, hard feelings persist.

Animosities develop between the contract cities and the county, too, with the most recent and serious concerning the pricing of services. Cost-conscious residents and officials of Lakewood and the other contract cities, acting jointly through the Contract Cities Association, have protested that they are paying too much. They are reluctant to pay overhead costs for services — costs they believe the county would have whether or not the services are contracted. They also point out that the system is inequitable because citizens of contract cities pay overhead costs twice — once through county taxes and again under the contract. In recent years, some cities have discontinued contracts — either for financial reasons or according to one city manager "because of public pressure to have our own program," adding that "citizens felt local personnel would have a better 'feel' for the community."[16] In 1971 Lakewood formed its own planning and building department. The next year it and several other contract cities began rethinking their contracts for police protection, in the wake of price increases. The contract with the Los Angeles Sheriff's Department assumes major importance because this constitutes the largest single budget item for most cities. According to Lakewood's mayor, "The city must work hard to provide the best service possible for its citizens at the lowest possible price. We have no preconception about the best place to do that. Experience has shown that, in many respects, it is with the county. But we do not hesitate to turn to private enterprise... or to provide our own services."[17]

The plan presents administrative problems for the county officials as well. They must remain flexible and ready to adjust personnel and equipment to the various levels of service requested by contract cities, and must station personnel and equipment to provide services to nonadjacent jurisdictions.

The extensiveness of Los Angeles County services raises

the question about how much counties should do. Mayors, council members and city managers from about 2500 cities were asked that question.[18] Most responded that counties should undertake new responsibilities for certain services traditionally offered by cities, plus some areawide functions. Others said counties should not be expected or asked to do any more than what they are doing now, unless their governing and administrative structures are modernized. The advocates of more active counties would have them beef up already existing services, especially by

stepping up their peace keeping operations
taking over tax-draining welfare programs
intensifying health services
supervising elections
assessing property and collecting taxes

Some functions city officials said they would not give up willingly were personnel services, maintenance of records and documents, controlling the supply and distribution of water, and recreation programs. The process of sorting out which government should do what promises to be an indefinite undertaking.

Pooling Resources to Serve the Public

Numerous cities and counties develop a more permanent arrangement for pooling resources by merging administrative departments to provide services countywide and to share the costs. Monroe County, New York claims to be one of the first, having combined many of its departments with the city of Rochester.[19] Welfare districts were the first to be merged (in 1947), followed by mutual responsibility for the airport, civil defense, training of firemen and mental health. By 1961 Monroe County and Rochester had a combined health department, a public safety laboratory and a 10,300 acre park system.

Then came a seven year delay caused by political differences — the city was controlled by one political party, the county by another. But in 1968, when the same party once again governed Rochester and Monroe County, consolidations resumed. A major goal was reached in 1971 when city and county civil service commissions were merged.

By entering contracts and merging departments local officials can successfully meet the demand for particular services, but cities and counties in a region are so interrelated and so many issues necessitating regional solutions arise, that there is a need to take a comprehensive overview. Several counties have a well defined geographic base, enabling their commissioners to take an overall perspective in planning for mass transit, highways, open space, airports, distribution of low cost housing, water supply, etc.; but many areas stretch beyond the boundaries of a single county, and another method for promoting a regional outlook is required. County and city officials have responded, due to concern for regional problems, fear of state intervention and prodding from the federal government, by creating councils of governments.

Councils of governments (commonly referred to as COGs and regional councils) are associations of cities and counties within a region. Each member government is represented in the council and its governing board by elected officials who meet regularly to discuss common problems, exchange information and develop a consensus on policy questions of mutual interest. Councils usually have additional duties: they develop areawide comprehensive plans, review applications for federal grants from members to ensure conformance with the plan, and serve as liaison to federal agencies. However, regional councils are associations, not governments. They cannot pass ordinances, they cannot enforce policies, they cannot implement regional land use plans. Despite this lack of power many COG policies are implemented voluntarily by

153

the region's cities and counties. Local governments in a region have the option of participating in the COG or not, but those deciding not to join may forfeit their right to apply for a variety of federal grants-in-aid. (See Chapter 7.)

Regional councils are relatively new types of organizations. A few were set up in the 1950s but most COGs were organized in the late 1960s. Supervisors (commissioners) of counties in the Detroit area are usually given credit for organizing the first one, known as the Supervisors Inter-County Committee (SICC). The committee owes its creation primarily to the president of the Wayne County Board of Supervisors (who also served on Detroit's city council). He foresaw some problems resulting from the rapid growth of the region with reference to adequate water supply, sewage and waste disposal, regional transportation — and was alarmed that the county supervisors were not attending to them. He met with officials of neighboring Macomb and Oakland Counties to discuss mutual problems and possible solutions; the meeting was fruitful, the SICC was organized officially and three other counties joined. Within a few years, the idea spread to other areas: New York City; Seattle; Rome, New York; Salem, Oregon; Washington, D.C.; and San Francisco to name a few.

Early councils of government were formed by county and city officials not only to promote cooperation and to coordinate activities, but to preempt state involvement in regional matters. ABAG, the Association of Bay Area Governments for the San Francisco area was established in 1961 because officials of the nine counties and several cities surrounding the bay believed the state would set up regional authorities and planning districts if they did not show some interest in facing metropolitan issues. Local officials in many areas created COGs as an alternative to political reorganization, such as the merger of the central city and the county or the creation of a new areawide government. By participating in regional councils, local officials could address areawide issues while preser-

154

ving their local city or county political base.

Essentially, issues of regional growth and development were not of top priority to city and county officials, and this attitude was reflected in the budgets and functions of the first COGs. They were financed by meager contributions from their members and private sources; their staffs were small and activities were limited to exchanging information and basic regional planning. The financial situation changed dramatically, as did the nature of regional councils, when in 1965 the federal government made them eligible for grants-in-aid for planning, and established planning requirements for cities and counties. The source of federal funds was the 701 planning program, which had financed planning operations of cities, counties, states and regional planning commissions since its enactment as part of the 1954 Housing Act. In 1965, when a new housing act was passed, the program was expanded to include councils of governments. For the first time, regional councils had access to substantial sources of income.

The following year, Congress passed the Demonstration Cities and Metropolitan Development Act. Section 204 made clear that if cities and counties wanted federal grants and loans for a variety of purposes, they must first submit their applications to an areawide planning agency for review and comment. Two years later, in Title IV of the Intergovernmental Cooperation Act, Congress reinforced its stand. The U.S. Bureau of the Budget (now the Office of Management and the Budget) was given responsibility for overseeing compliance with the planning requirements; in 1969 it issued Circular A-95, which stated that grant applications from cities and counties should be submitted to a "regional clearinghouse" — essentially a COG — for comment and review before being sent to the federal agency for funding. Failure to set up a clearinghouse or to submit grant applications to it would mean that cities and counties could not apply for a host of federal grants, primarily those subsidizing construction of public facilities. The result of these acts is clearly shown in the jump in the number of councils of governments. Thirty-five councils existed in 1965, according to the National Association of Regional Councils; two years later there were 103 and by 1972 there were 352. Federal interest in COGs is not limited to urban areas. Economic development districts established as a result of the 1965 Public Works and Economic Development Act perform the functions of a regional council in rural sections of the country.

Since 1965, the purposes of regional councils have expanded from associations developed by city and county officials to promote coordination and cooperation to organizations charged with carrying out federal policy. At times these two purposes conflict, and because councils rely so heavily on federal financial support, local priorities are often displaced by federal ones. In the view of political scientist Henry J. Schmandt:

> COGs are kept busy, on the one hand, trying to demonstrate to federal authorities that they are worthwhile investments and, on the other, reassuring local units that they constitute no threat to them.

Local and federal officials realize the values of regional councils in developing a regional perspective, but many of them are doubtful that these organizations will be able to keep up with areawide problems and reconcile conflicts between federal and local officials and among city and county leaders unless given the authority to enforce decisions and operate programs — in short, unless they become regional governments.

Some cities and counties have formed new political systems, essentially regional governments, by reorganization. There are two basic approaches which have been taken:

> The county is reorganized, usually under a charter, simultaneously assuming new powers and responsibilities which make it legally superior to the cities (only Dade County to date).
> Most county functions are assumed by the central city

under a new consolidated government. The county remains to handle a few state mandated responsibilities. In a variation of this scheme, the county takes over responsibilities under a joint city-county government.

Dade County Reorganization

In 1957, voters of Dade County, Florida adopted a powerful charter revamping the county governing structure, and establishing it as the principal government of the area by giving it power to regulate some municipal activities and transferring to it some city responsibilities.[20] Before that time, citizens of the county lived under a governmental system similar to that found in most other parts of Florida and the nation. Dade had the traditional form of government: a board of five commissioners, ten independently elected administrators, fourteen elected judges, five elected constables, and five elected justices of the peace. Each commissioner built a strong personal following with patronage and authority to let contracts. Some were extremely successful, staying in office for more than 20 years. The county was not authorized to perform urban services, with the exception of a few specifically designated by the state, despite the fact that nearly half of the county residents lived in unincorporated areas. Other citizens looked to both the county and one of 27 cities for public services.

Each of the 27 cities was proud of its independence, but pride was no obstacle to cooperating with one another or with the county when necessary. Informal agreements, contracts, even the merger of some departments and the transfer of some city functions to the county, were developed to provide a higher quality of public service on an areawide basis. There was cooperation in the sale and distribution of water, training of policemen, fire fighting, sick care, public education, and a few other areas.

Some of the cooperative ventures were long overdue. Prior to the creation of a county-wide school system in 1945, Dade was divided into ten school districts, with boundaries crisscrossing municipal lines. Minimum standards were set for the entire county but rarely enforced because some districts could not afford them. What money the school districts had was deposited in 28 separate bank accounts, drawn on with checks of 28 different colors.

The police emergency communication system also was a victim of fragmentation. Six systems existed. When an emergency developed, the Miami Emergency Radio Network notified dispatchers in various parts of the county who contacted other dispatchers, who finally relayed the message to their respective mobile units.

Mutual programs were a response to public demands for quality services and to the need for a county-wide tax base. The Jackson Memorial Hospital, for example, was transferred from Miami to the county because the city could no longer carry the operating costs or meet the continuing need for modern equipment—a situation forcefully brought home to voters when several babies died in a diarrhea epidemic in 1948.

During the years of piecemeal attempts to develop intergovernmental cooperation and a county-wide approach to public services, civic interests, especially the Miami Chamber of Commerce and the *Miami Herald,* called for a complete overhaul of the political system. Fifteen years of unsuccessful attempts culminated in 1957 when the Dade County charter was adopted.

The charter gave Dade County powers seldom proposed for counties:

> Responsibility to provide countywide some municipal services, including housing and slum clearance and power to control development through comprehensive planning, zoning, building codes, regulation of waste and sewage, and water supply

Responsibility to provide a full array of urban services to citizens of unincorporated areas.

Authority to create new municipalities from unincorporated areas, after appropriate hearings and an affirmative vote by the residents of that area, and authority to approve annexations.

Responsibility to set minimum service standards for cities and to take over services if the standards are not met. Cities may request that the county assume additional functions or the county board may ask citizens of cities, through a special election, if they prefer the county to the city service. As part of the authority to set minimum standards the county can regulate the sale of alcoholic beverages, a power with implications for tourist centers such as Miami Beach.

In a complete reversal of the traditional Dillon Rule, Dade County may exercise all the powers and privileges granted to cities, as well as to counties, by the state constitution and laws. Furthermore, the charter declares that the powers enumerated in the charter are not exclusive or restrictive, but should be interpreted to include all implied powers necessary and proper to carrying out the county's assignments. A "supremacy" clause makes the charter superior to all municipal charters and ordinances, except in certain specified cases.

The charter was not all one-sided; certain limits were placed on the county and the cities were given guarantees. The document assures that:

The municipalities ... shall remain in existence so long as their electors desire. No municipality ... shall be abolished without approval of a majority of its electors. ... The right of self-determination in local affairs is reserved and preserved to the municipalities except as otherwise provided in this charter.[21]

Municipalities still operate under their own charters.

The new system of government delegated strong powers to the reorganized Dade County but the charter did not provide the necessary authority to execute all of them. It did not provide for strong, unified leadership, although the new government form provided for a manager and abolished several elected row offices.[22] Dade is now governed by a board of eight commissioners nominated from districts but elected at large plus a mayor who is the permanent commission chairman. The mayor has no specific executive powers. Being the only governing board member nominated and elected at large, the mayor could assume political leadership by force of personality and as symbolic head of the government, but men holding the office to date have preferred a low profile. Apparently, Dade County residents want it that way: in 1972 they defeated by a two-to-one margin a charter amendment to create the office of elected county executive.

Administrative matters are assigned to a county manager appointed by the board. County commissioners and citizens expect this official to fill the leadership gap, but when managers become too involved, stepping beyond the tenuous boundary dividing administration from politics, they are dismissed.

The county's power to raise money is not as strong as it needs to be.[23] Under the charter, Dade County is expected to provide more and better services, but its taxing powers remain the same, forcing continued reliance on the property tax. The Florida constitution requires that all sections of the county, unincorporated as well as incorporated, be taxed at the same rate. The equal rate was fair when Dade provided the same services to all residents, but under the new charter it gives special treatment to the half of the county residents who live in unincorporated areas because they are provided with both countywide and municipal services. City residents have been understandably upset. The county has taken steps to equate expenses by imposing some special, non-property taxes on

160

residents of unincorporated areas, under permission recently granted by the state, but the problem persists. In 1971 the Dade County Metropolitan Study Commission suggested that the urbanized unincorporated areas be divided into service districts to provide local services and to finance local needs.

The fiscal problems have prevented Dade from enforcing the minimum service standards provided for by the charter. The county simply does not have the funds to take over services from a delinquent city. Political realities and the strength of the cities have curtailed the county's control over city planning and zoning at a time when many area residents regard further development as a threat (see Chapter 3). The county does zone for 43 percent of Dade's residents living in unincorporated communities, but its authority in cities is based on persuasion. Soon after the charter became operative, Dade officials tried to exercise their full zoning powers by virtually eliminating city authority. Draft ordinances spelling out the expanded county powers, highly criticized by the cities, were modified in the cities' favor and the implementation date was extended several times. Finally they were adopted, but the zoning ordinances were repealed in 1958. The issue came up again in 1971 when the metropolitan study commission recommended that the Dade charter be amended to permit county review of city zoning changes when they deviated from the county comprehensive land use plan.

Dade County has not been able to exert the degree of authority outlined by the charter in the crucial areas of water supply or sewage disposal. However, it successfully enforces a building code countywide and has passed a subdivision ordinance controlling development of vacant land. Dade has been more successful in its housing programs, which are administered by its department of housing and urban development, known as "little HUD," created in 1963. Low income housing projects have been placed in various sections of the county, after negotiation with municipal officials.

Amid the conflicts—which may never be resolved to

anyone's satisfaction—the new government in Dade County has accomplished many things: the county administrative operations are centralized and modern; there are stringent air and water pollution control regulations; all properties are assessed by the county in a uniform manner; and a community relations board works to ease racial tensions.

Merging City and County Governments

A different approach has been developed by cities and counties in 21 areas: the central city and smaller municipalities have been merged with the county to form a single government.[24] In most of these arrangements a remnant of county government continues to operate apart from the consolidated unit to carry out state-mandated functions, and a few small municipalities have chosen not to be included in the plan; but essentially the consolidated government combines the county and city departments and governing apparatus.

City-county consolidation has intrigued political scientists, civic reformers and local officials since the early 1800s, but voters have responded to the concept only recently—and many remain skeptical. Half of the 21 mergers now in effect have been approved since 1960. Civic and political leaders have shown more interest in studying the idea than in adopting it, and today more than 30 areas are giving the merger plan "careful consideration."[25] If history serves as a guide, every area studying a merger will propose some type of political integration, and again, if history is a guide very few will follow through, at least not the first time. Since 1949, only 10 of 36 proposed consolidation plans have won at the polls. Tampa and Hillsborough, Florida have proposed a merger to voters three times since 1967, without success; Macon and Bibb County, Georgia attempted consolidation unsuccessfully in 1933, 1960 and 1972.[26]

162

With the long list of failures, it seems remarkable that four areas adopted consolidated governments in the 1800s: New Orleans (1813), Boston (1821), Philadelphia (1854), and New York (1898). However, the animosities separating cities, counties, and suburbs today began to surface in the 1900s. Suburbanites developed strong attachments to their small communities; arguments of efficiency and economy fell on deaf ears. Opposition to consolidation was reflected in state laws and constitutions, which were either silent on the issue or prohibited it. In states where constitutions had no merger provisions, coalitions of rural and suburban legislators refused to consider them. Many of these legal barriers to merger remain, and in areas where the city and county wish to merge, the state constitution usually has to be amended, requiring a vote by all the people of the state.

One area, Baton Rouge, did not succumb to the obstacles, and the city and parish adopted a new governing plan in 1947. The Baton Rouge plan did not disturb the boundaries of the existing governments. It set up interlocking governing bodies: the seven city council members are also the parish council, along with two other members elected from rural sections of the area. The mayor-president, elected at large, is the head of both governments and appoints the heads of operating departments which serve both. The parish council appoints some traditional county officers—the clerk and treasurer, for example. The governments are integrated, but have some flexibility; there are separate budgets and accounting systems, and some separate boards and commissions.

Fifteen years passed before another area adopted an integrated political system; then Nashville and Davidson County did so in 1962. Since then, interest in city-county merger has increased substantially, because of the same economic and political reasons causing the revitalization of counties generally. Take Jacksonville-Duval County, Florida for example. The population skyrocketed from 210,000 in the mid-

163

1940s to more than half a million by the mid-1960s; and neither Jacksonville nor the county could keep up. The revitalization of the area, so desperately needed after years of neglect during the depression and World War II, was slow in coming. Finally the roof fell in. In 1964, after repeated threats, the Southern Association of Colleges and Schools disaccredited all 15 high schools in the county; conditions were ripe for a major epidemic because of soil and water contamination from 30,000 septic tanks used by 120,000 people, and the St. Johns River had been polluted by 80 percent of Jacksonville's raw sewage. The air was polluted; neither the city nor the county offered adequate police and fire protection; and as a final blow, city and county officials were indicted for larceny, conspiracy and perjury.[27] A study commission convened, the state legislature was persuaded to grant the necessary authority, and in 1967 the consolidated Jacksonville-Duval County government began operation.

Reform is not always surrounded by such calamities. Sometimes it is promoted by civic interests to eliminate duplication of services, and to take advantage of economies of scale. In other areas there were inconveniences, health hazards, lack of planning, and contradictory as it may first appear, a desire by county officials to maintain political status quo.

It is difficult to change a political system. Many counties have tried relatively minor adjustments and have failed. Merging a city and county is even more difficult. First there are legal obstacles. In many states, the legislature must approve formation of a local government study commission, and then the idea must receive the approval of voters. A constitutional amendment may be necessary to authorize city-county consolidation and voters throughout the state have to approve it. Finally the consolidation plan must be submitted to local voters. There are also human obstacles. Current officeholders and bureaucrats fear loss of their jobs or of political power; citizens fear loss of autonomy or dilution of voting strength. Everyone is wary of higher taxes. Considering

164

these barriers what accounts for the successful mergers? The following case study of Lexington-Fayette County points out a few factors.

Lexington-Fayette County Merger

The successful Lexington-Fayette County, Kentucky merger is a case study of carefully thought out political action.[28] Utilizing compromises, cajolery, persuasion, great energy and just plain luck, the proponents of city-county consolidation came forward with their plan at precisely the right time in the area's history. November 7, 1970, voters in the city and county approved the charter by better than a two-to-one margin.

The impetus for merger began in the Kentucky legislature. Before 1970, Kentucky state law forbade governmental consolidation, although some functional mergers were permitted through contractual arrangements. In that year, two state legislators from Lexington drew up a bill permitting full governmental consolidation for counties with cities of a particular size, drafting the law not because of constituent pressure but because one of the men "felt very strongly about it—that merger should at least not be forbidden to urbanizing counties." Their bill became law.

The timing was right for political change in Lexington and the county. All residents were growing weary of the city's piecemeal annexations, producing a city map described as a "civic Rorschach test" by one local merger proponent, and leading to disputes over jurisdiction. One story relates that a man lay on the street with four bullets in him while a county policeman and a city policeman argued whether he was in the city or the unincorporated county. Some citizens were apprehensive when a court decision cleared the way for Lexington to abandon the bit-by-bit approach and annex large chunks of the county by 1975 or 1980, yet the county fell short of taking care of urban needs, operating instead as a "storekeeper, meant only to serve a rural area."[29]

Soon after the state law was passed, the local League of Women Voters circulated a petition to set up a merger commission. Members of the fiscal court (the county governing body) were among the first to sign. Unlike officials in many counties and cities who fear reorganizations, the Fayette County commissioners remained vigorous supporters of consolidation throughout the merger campaign.

A commission was established and after months of work it developed a plan for combining the city and county governments. The next and most difficult step was to urge voters to approve it. Merger proponents launched a vigorous campaign. First they appealed to community leaders, convincing them of the values of consolidation. One campaigner explained why.

We knew that 99 percent of the people would not read the charter or attend public hearings on it. We also knew that a charter has no personality of its own. But we used peer group influence to elicit the reaction 'if so-and-so is for it, it must be okay'.[30]

Second, they studied consolidation attempts in other areas to identify factors accounting for success or failure. Some of the key campaigners were experienced politicians who knew the county well. They sensed which part of the charter to emphasize in which district and who to send to talk about it. For the black districts they emphasized better representation and sent the acting city manager, a black, to talk. In suburban areas they reminded residents of the pending annexation and the duplication of services under the present system. All merger proponents felt rural residents could not be persuaded to support reorganization so they didn't try.

In the end the charter lost only in six districts, five of them rural. The combined government took over January 1,

166

1974 under the leadership of an urban county mayor, 15 councilmen, and a chief administrative officer.

There may have been a time when cities and counties limited their activities to their state-assigned roles, cities to serve local needs and counties to carry out state policies, but no longer. Now local governments in many places consider their first responsibility to be to local citizens. Counties are beginning to act like cities, providing a wide array of services and even assuming some formerly offered by cities. Municipalities, originally created as service agencies and political units, are now being established solely for political reasons—to give residents small town government in a big town setting. Meanwhile, the need for government—to offer services and to manage community conflicts—is growing.

Both competition and cooperation between cities and counties have resulted. Competition has developed over what functions each local government should assume and over how much social responsibility their constituents have for other parts of the region. Cooperation has developed when cities and counties have realized the task of governing has become too immense to be handled alone.

Distributing the governmental work load is difficult because it is not merely the mechanical process of assigning one group of functions to cities, another to counties, and a third to suburbs. Although it has been maintained that counties, encompassing more land and constituents, should be responsible for areawide functions, leaving the more immediate local functions to cities, no criteria for distinguishing areawide from local have been developed.

In essence, responsibilities will be distributed and accommodations will be reached through politics. The forms of cooperation will vary from informal agreements to political amalgamation, and relationships will shift with need and political reality.

Notes

1. Torrence, Susan W., *Super City-Home Town, U.S.A.* (New York: Praeger Publishers, 1974).

2. Schmandt, Henry J., John C. Goldbach and Donald B. Vogel, *Milwaukee: A Contemporary Urban Profile* (New York: Praeger Publishers, 1971), p. 179.

3. Torrence, *op. cit.*

4. Schmandt, Goldbach, and Vogel, *op. cit.*

5. "Twin Cities," *City,* January-February 1971.

6. Jennings, Bill, "Nonmetropolitan Area Cooperation Is a Necessity, Too," *Nation's Cities,* vol. 10, no. 11, November 1972, p. 19.

7. *Ibid.*

8. Advisory Commission on Intergovernmental Relations, *The Challenge of Local Government Reorganization* (Washington, D.C.: U.S. Government Printing Office, forthcoming).

9. Stoner, John E. *Interlocal Governmental Cooperation: A Study of Five States.* Agriculture Economic Report No. 118 (Washington, D.C.: U.S. Department of Agriculture, July 1967), p. 5.

10. Advisory Commission on Intergovernmental Relations, *Profile of County Government* (Washington, D.C.: U.S. Government Printing Office, 1972), p. 25.

11. *Constitution of the State of New York,* art. IX, sec. 1(c).

12. Grosenick, Leigh E., *A Manual for Interlocal Cooperation in Minnesota* (St. Paul: Office of Local and Urban Affairs, State Planning Agency, May 1969), p. 113.

13. Advisory Commission on Intergovernmental Relations, *The Challenge of Local Government Reorganization.*

14. Advisory Commission on Intergovernmental Relations, *Profile of County Government,* p. 26.

15. Information on Los Angeles County was obtained

168

from the following: Bollens, John C. and Henry J. Schmandt, *The Metropolis: Its People, Politics, and Economic Life,* 2nd ed. (New York: Harper and Row, Publishers, 1970); Ries, John C. and John J. Kirlin, "Government in the Los Angeles Area: The Issue of Centralization and Decentralization, in-*Los Angeles: Viability and Prospects for Metropolitan Leadership,* Werner Z. Hirsch, ed. (New York: Praeger Publishers, 1971); Mogulof, Melvin B., *Five Metropolitan Governments* (Washington, D.C.: The Urban Institute, 1972); "Contract Cities Program Today," Remarks before "New County, U.S.A." Conference of the National Association of Counties, Atlanta, Georgia, July 1970; Torrence, Susan W., *Super City-Home Town, U.S.A.* (New York: Praeger Publishers, 1974).

16. Torrence, *op. cit.*

17. *Ibid.*

18. Advisory Commission on Intergovernmental Relations. *The Challenge of Local Government Reorganization.*

19. "Functional Consolidations," mimeograph, National Association of Counties.

20. Information on Dade County based on Sofen, Edward, *The Miami Metropolitan Experiment,* 2nd ed. (Garden City, New York: Anchor Books, 1966); Bollens and Schmandt, *op. cit.;* and Torrence, *op. cit.*

21. Dade County Charter, article 5, sections 5.01-5.05.

22. Sofen, *op. cit.*

23. *Ibid.*

24. Marando, Vincent L., "Local Governmental Reorganization: An Overview," Prepared for the National Academy of Public Administration, Washington, D.C., November 7, 1972.

25. National Association of Counties staff.

26. Marando, *op. cit.*

27. Martin, Richard, *Consolidation: Jacksonville-Duval County* (Jacksonville, Florida: Crawford Publishing Company, 1968), p. xi-47.

28. Zeller, Florence, "Merger in the Blue Grass," *New County Times,* December 1972.

29. *Ibid.*

30. *Ibid.*

7. The Impact of the Federal Government

The powers not delegated to the United States by the Constitution, nor prohibited by it to the States, are reserved to the States respectively, or to the people . . *Article X, Constitution of the United States.*

Article X establishes the distribution of powers among levels of government in this country. There is no mention of local government. Constitutionally the 3000 counties, which spend billions, employ millions, care for the sick, administer welfare, provide recreational opportunities, build expressways, prevent crime in the streets, and render countless other services, are not recognized. Nor are their colleagues, the cities. Theoretically the national government has no relationship with counties or cities, but only with the states which created them, and for about 150 years the federal government, abiding by this constitutional formality, did not deal directly with local governments. In fact *City Government in the United States,* Frank Goodnow's pioneering textbook written in 1904, stated that "as the city has no relations with the national government it is not necessary for our purpose that we make any study of the national administrative system."[1]

However, the Constitution has been sufficiently ambiguous to encourage the federal government to test its powers, and since infancy it has been flexing its muscles. Article X has not been amended since it was written in 1787, but like other sections its meaning has been revised to suit the tenor of the times. A major restructuring of federal-state-local relations occurred during the 1930s when strict interpretations of the Constitution gave way to the realities of a nationwide depression. Conscious of the need for centralized leadership and using its superior money-raising power, along with a liberal interpretation of fiscal authority, the federal government quickly moved to provide health and social welfare services formerly provided by the states and localities. Furthermore, by giving loans and subsidies for housing and other community development projects, it began dealing directly with local governments to achieve its objectives.

The depression was only one factor in the increasing involvement of the federal government in community affairs. The development of modern communications and transportation increasingly integrated the country, along with an economy growing more national in scope. Local problems became national and vice versa. For example, dumping untreated sewage in a stream is a local problem until it occurs in every locality, then it becomes a nationwide issue. Wars are settled by the federal government, but closed defense plants flood county welfare rolls.

Today there are numerous and powerful links between the federal and local governments, and usually the state is involved. Especially since the 1960s the federal government has become increasingly active in education, economic development, elimination of poverty, law enforcement and other functions once regarded as exclusively local. Money is the key, which is understandable when one compares the federal government's power to raise funds and its willingness to spend to that of states and localities. At the outset of this century, over 60 percent of the tax revenues of all governments was raised by state and local authorities. Sixty years later nearly

70 percent of the total was collected at the national level, and the trend has continued since.[2] The federal government gives substantial portions of its revenue to counties, cities and states through grants and loans. The purpose is to have federal funds applied locally to meet nationally defined domestic goals. County officials welcome additional money, in many cases depend on it, but they are not always enthusiastic about the way it is distributed or the conditions put on its use. Often this financial assistance has enabled the federal government to influence county policies, spending patterns, and administration. The resulting conflicts are a great part of federal-county relations.

The federal government has final authority in determining how its funds will be distributed and spent. However, federal officials—members of Congress and the executive branch—cannot dictate to county officials. If federal leaders want localities to curb water pollution or operate day care centers for welfare mothers among a host of national priorities, they must present programs which are attractive to those who will implement them.

The Fiscal Impact of the Federal Government

The federal government distributes substantial amounts of money to the other levels of government through an elaborate system of grants-in-aid. County officials, like their state and city counterparts, receive most of their federal money under two types of grants: categorical grants and revenue sharing (initiated in 1972 by the Nixon administration as part of the effort to revise the grant system).

In fiscal 1973 the federal government pumped about $43.5 billion (including about $5 billion in general revenue sharing) into states and localities through grants. In fiscal 1974 the grant budget was $48 billion, and in fiscal 1975 it will be $51.7 billion (see graph page 174). Federal authoriza-

173

tions for grants-in-aid have increased by more than 700 percent since 1960.[3] All told, grants pay for about 20 percent of state and local expenses, although the actual proportion varies from year to year.[4] Grants represent only a portion of county budgets, but they often provide the margin needed to get some jobs done (frequently without raising property taxes), plus some leeway for research and development.

Federal Grants to State and Local Governments

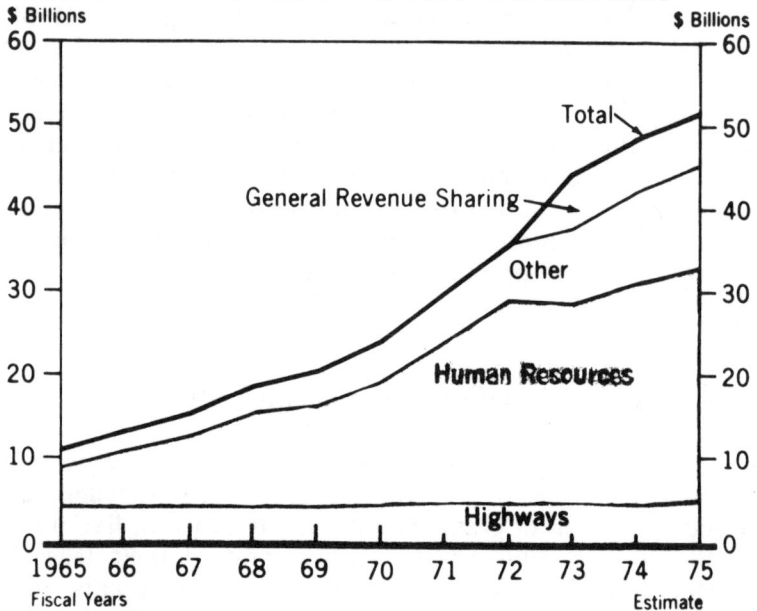

Source: *The United States Budget in Brief,* U.S.G.P.O., 1974

Grants have also grown as a proportion of the federal budget—from 9 percent of the total federal outlay in fiscal 1965 to 17 percent in fiscal 1975; 25 percent of all federal funds spent on domestic programs are allocated to grants.[5]

The lion's share of federal aid comes through categorical grants, so called because the money must be used for a specific program, e.g. hot lunches for the elderly, and because the program must be managed according to federal specifications. Categorical grants are further subdivided into project grants and formula grants. Project grants are the most numerous and familiar to the general public. Designed to meet a specific need, they are allocated through national competition. Counties, cities and for some programs, states apply directly to the federal government for funds. The money is used for research, planning, training, construction, or experimentation with new techniques in a vast array of activities from caring for children to killing rats.

Under formula grants (similar to block grants) monies are given usually to states, according to criteria such as fiscal capacity, population, number of poor, etc. These funds are distributed automatically, without application, but they must be used for a specified purpose. States in turn usually distribute these funds to counties and cities, but the local governments must apply for them and comply with state and federal requirements.

The 1000 or more separate grant programs support a variety of services in every functional field. Most of the money—nearly $21 billion or 40 percent in fiscal 1975—is dispensed by the Department of Health, Education, and Welfare which operates at least 300 grants-in-aid. Most of the HEW funds are used for income maintenance—aid to families with dependent children, assistance to the aged, blind and disabled, and so on. The following chart shows the outlays of federal grant funds by function and department for fiscal 1973; although the numbers have changed, the relative allocations remain the same for fiscal 1975. In varying degrees either directly or through the states, counties have been able to count on grants to relieve their tight budgets since the first monetary grant program began in 1875. Through the years some county officials proudly refused to apply for or ac-

175

Distribution of Federal Grants-in-Aid

Outlays by Function

billions of dollars, fiscal 1973 est.

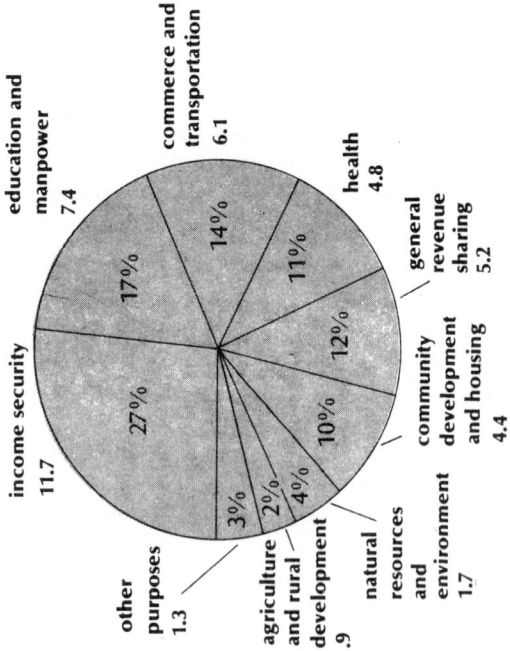

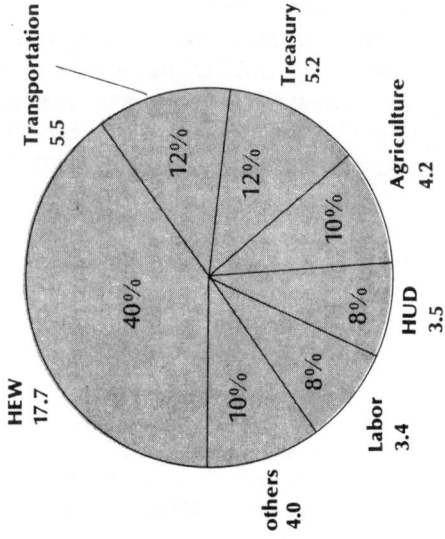

education and manpower
7.4

commerce and transportation
6.1

health
4.8

general revenue sharing
5.2

income security
11.7

27%

17%

14%

11%

12%

10%

4%

2%

3%

community development and housing
4.4

other purposes
1.3

agriculture and rural development
.9

natural resources and environment
1.7

Outlays by Department

billions of dollars, fiscal 1973 est.

Transportation
5.5

Treasury
5.2

Agriculture
4.2

HEW
17.7

40%

12%

12%

10%

10%

8%

8%

HUD
3.5

Labor
3.4

others
4.0

SOURCE: Office of Management and Budget

cept "tainted" federal funds, but today incumbents are voted out of office because their rivals accuse them of failing to get their county a full share of the federal largesse. Officials generally follow the advice of the National Association of Counties:

> While it is easy to find fault with the grant-in-aid system, or with an individual grant program, time spent focusing on these faults or refusal to use grants will not help officials serve their county better.[6]

In effect grants-in-aid enable county officials to recoup some of their constituents' federal income taxes and put them to work locally. Those who do not enter the grants contest or who fail to win federal assistance will have to use local taxes to fund projects which may be undertaken with federal subsidies by other counties.

Federal funds also give counties room for experimentation. In fiscal 1973 over $13 million was set aside to underwrite new approaches in curbing drug abuse; the Law Enforcement Assistance Administration was scheduled to award about $150 million of its 1974 authorization to selected local governments wanting to test new techniques for reducing street crime and burglaries. The Department of Transportation, in fiscal 1974, was authorized $50 million in experimental funds for developing methods for safer state and county roads.[7] Even grant programs not specifically allocated for experimentation can promote new ideas through the competition among local governments for funds. Often it is the best idea which wins the grant, not necessarily the county with the greatest need.

County commissioners apply for grants to ease local financial strains, but forethought plus experience teaches that, in ways sometimes anticipated and others quite unexpected, grants also cost money. Most grants require a commitment of local funds; the proportion varies widely from program to program. Some require all recipients to pay a

177

matching proportion of the total program cost; others vary the obligation according to the jurisdiction's ability to pay. Payment is required in hard cash for some programs, or "in kind"—services or property—for others. On the average, counties pay from 25 percent to 40 percent of the total project costs for federally funded programs. In 1966, according to the National Association of Counties, state and local governments spent $5.5 billion to match $13 billion in federal funds, and it is estimated that they spend one dollar to match every two and a half dollars from the federal government today.[8] In recent years 10 to 14 percent of all locally raised dollars have been spent to match federal grants.[9] The federal government now allows counties and other recipients to recoup some indirect costs associated with implementing funded projects, but not all federal agencies have been given their share of the money to make good on local charges against them.

The proportion of the project cost the federal government will pay is usually set for each categorical grant program by Congress, or more specifically, by various congressional committees. Until the 1930s Congress required that project costs be divided equally between the federal government and the recipient states; during the depression years when several new grants were authorized, the general practice was to base matching requirements on the state or local need for the program and the ability to pay. Another change was made in the 1950s with the enactment of the Interstate Highway Act when the federal government agreed to pick up 90 percent of the program costs because the system of national highways was deemed essential for the nation's security. Since that time each congressional committee with authority over a categorical program has acted independently, setting the respective financial requirements for the federal government and the states and localities according to its own prerogatives, with little or no coordination with other committees and without much guidance from the executive branch. Often, matching requirements reflect the committee's interpretation

178

of national goals, calling for the federal government to pay a generous proportion of the costs for top priorities. In recent years the federal government has contributed well over half of the monies for water pollution control, construction of waste treatment plants, operation of day care centers for children of welfare mothers, and improvement of police programs. In addition to national priorities, Congress seems willing to commit the federal government to a high percentage of project costs to encourage local governments to initiate new services and to undertake demonstration or pilot programs.

County officials expect to pay a portion of the cost of federally supported programs, but other expenses develop unexpectedly. The lengthy application process and the uncertainty of whether a grant will be awarded put county officials in an awkward budgeting position. The county must be ready to begin work when an application is approved; this often requires preliminary local action, tying up funds which could be used elsewhere. The mayor-president of the Baton Rouge-East Baton Rouge Parish faced such a plight in trying to obtain funds for a downtown renewal project. The city-parish cleared some property it owned for a civic center with the understanding from the housing and and urban affairs department that federal support would be forthcoming in a short time. Nearly a year later formal approval was granted, and the city-parish was reimbursed for some of its expenses. But in the meantime, lamented Mayor-President Woodrow Dumas,

> We were using our own money, which we borrowed. It just cost us a ton of money. We spent six, eight, ten, eleven months working on a project application, and we still don't know whether we'll get it or not.[10]

County commissioners face financial problems when grants terminate, as well as when they start. Most federally sponsored programs are funded for one to three years. Afterwards, commissioners must decide to discontinue a program which

179

may be popular with some segments of the community or absorb the costs into the total county budget which may be stretched to its limits already. This problem is becoming more acute because the Nixon administration is attempting to discontinue many grant programs and trim the funds for others.

Beyond Money: The Impact on Decisions
and Administration

The impact of the grant system is not confined to money. It influences the way county officials govern their communities, especially their selection of program priorities and the administration of those programs. County commissioners and executives are encouraged to seek the federal dollar. Frequently they destroy local priorities to do so, often at great expense. Kent County, Michigan is a good example. There was need for a new jail which could not be financed completely on a local basis. This resulted in a determined effort to secure federal funds to expand the local budget. The outcome, however, was a new library, with help from the Department of Health, Education, and Welfare, and additional money from HEW to build mental health outpatient clinics. Now the county is strapped for funds to operate its new facilities, and it is still without its jail.[11] The executive of Marin County, California, who has had similar experiences, put it this way: "If you are looking for federal dollars, you have to find a narrow federal slot with the money, and then fit whatever local problems you have to the slot."[12]

Why do such disruptions occur? In part because of pressure from federal bureaucrats who have an obvious stake in the success of their own programs; careers ride on the success stories that the administrators can take to Congress at budget appropriation time or to the Office of Management and Budget, which actually controls disbursement of funds. Thus, there is a search for recipients, especially counties which have done well with government grants in the past. County officials, flattered at being asked to apply, would find it hard to tell their benefactors that the project doesn't fit this year's local priorities.

Another answer is that national priorities do not result always in a proper fit at the local level. Grant programs, especially those enacted during the 1960s, were developed to meet national needs. The model cities program was enacted because "Congress hereby finds and declares that improving the quality of urban life is the most critical domestic problem facing the United States." The Area Redevelopment Act was passed because "The Congress declares that the maintenance of the national economy at a high level is vital to the best interests of the United States," and the Economic Opportunity Act was passed because "The United States can achieve its full economic and social potential as a nation only if every individual has the opportunity to contribute to the full extent of his capabilities and to participate in the workings of our society."[13]

The explicit declaration of national objectives implies that the county commissioners taking part in the program are doing so in the national interest, not in the community interest. From the start, it is assumed that the policies established by the county government are secondary to the purposes of the federal grants which are being sought to finance them.

Appointed county officials usually assume important roles in applying for and administering grants. Unless their efforts are well-supervised and coordinated, it is hard for elected policy-makers to keep abreast of the federal funds coming into the county, the county resources needed to match them, and the programs they support.

Cities are no different. After a lengthy study of the grant-in-aid system in Richmond, Virginia, a study team from the Office of Management and Budget concluded that no one actually knew how much federal money flowed into the city or where it went. The team identified $30.7 million of 1970 disbursements to the city, 11 percent of the budget for that year, but conceded that, like most state and local budget and accounting systems, there was a failure to reflect the true extent of federal funding. It took the mayor of San Jose, California a year and $200,000 of federal funds to track down the city departments receiving federal grants and to ascertain the total amount the city had received.[14]

Allen E. Pritchard, Jr., executive vice president of the National League of Cities, explained how appointed officials can assume authority:

> The categorical system builds bureaucracies . . . within the state and local governments . . . to the point where it is impossible for a mayor and a city council to make a realistic policy. They [the elected officials] are always up against the wall because independent agencies learn to play the ball game on these categorical grants, and they are always coming in at five minutes to twelve and saying, "We've got to sign off on this application or we aren't going to get the money," or "We don't have any options because if we do it the way we want to do it, we can't get the money."[15]

Appointed officials have taken the lead in obtaining federal grants for some of the same reasons they acquired relatively powerful positions in local decision making. They are on the job all the time, and they are professionals, the elected governing board members are neither. Department heads who want more funds for their departments naturally are aggressive in looking to the federal government or to state agencies administering federal programs, and, in many cases, governing board members simply do not take the time to supervise their activities in order to keep abreast with the latest developments.

The search for funds leads county department heads to the program administrators in Washington or the state capital where they usually find fellow professionals in the same functional area; they often establish good rapport or even close professional relationships. By the same token, federal and state program administrators would prefer to deal with their local, professional counterparts, rather than with the elected officials who, they are sure, know little about the technicalities of, say, designing safer roads. The Senate Subcommittee on Intergovernmental Relations surveyed the attitudes of federal grant program administrators; it detected a "preoccupation with protecting and promoting the purposes of their individual programs" and "hostilities between professional program administrators and elected policy makers at all levels of government."[16]

On the other hand, effective county commissioners can strengthen their governments through aggressive department heads who know their federal and state colleagues. These persons can be alert to the county's specific needs and on the watch for federal programs to help with the financing. In general, those grant programs which strengthen appointed officials can also strengthen county commissioners if they exert strong leadership.

Even when county commissioners aggressively assert themselves, develop program priorities, direct their department heads to seek federal funding to meet those priorities, and then keep a record of the grants actually applied for and received, there is still trouble. The number and variety of federal grant programs is staggering. Just perusing the list in search of useful and pertinent programs can be a full-time job, when one considers that there are over 1000 from which to choose. Furthermore, organization and categorization at the federal level is lacking. The Labor Department, for example, administers programs to train the poor for jobs in the private sector. Instead of assembling their activities into an appropriate category, the Department operates separate programs for teenagers, elderly, blacks, Chicanos, Indians, and welfare clients. At one point, similarly, the federal government distributed grants for sewer and water projects under

183

three separate programs available from three different agencies with three different matching requirements. It ran eight separate programs for libraries and two for historic preservation. Thus, if there is confusion at the local level, much of it reflects the confusion at the national level.

To make the grant program more comprehensible, many federal agencies and public interest groups have compiled catalogues of all the grant programs. Though the intent is to assemble a comprehensive list, some programs invariably are missing. In 1966 the Advisory Commission on Intergovernmental Relations (ACIR) developed a "catalogue of catalogues"—a bibliography of information sources for grants. The first edition and its supplement were eighteen pages long![17] Currently the catalogue considered to be most complete is the *Catalogue of Federal Domestic Assistance,* compiled and updated annually by the federal government.

The Impact on Organization

Because of the assumed primacy of national goals, the federal government has insisted that the grant programs be administered according to certain specifications. County commissioners find that, if they want to participate, they must meet a variety of qualifications, some even requiring administrative reorganization and hiring of new personnel. The requirement for planning is a good example. In addition to conformity with state plans, many grants require local project plans. Furthermore, they stipulate that local plans must conform to a functional or a comprehensive areawide plan, or both. County applications for transportation funds, for example, have to comply with an areawide transportation plan and an areawide comprehensive plan, as do applications for solid waste disposal, open space preservation, mass transportation and basic sewer and water services. In fact, the planning requirements became so complex at one point that the direc-

184

tor of the Bureau of the Budget noted:

> Certain planning requirements necessarily demanded as a condition of grants may be overlapping. This duplication can defeat the very purpose for which planning is sought ... In some areas we may be overplanning, while serious planning gaps exist elsewhere.[18]

Counties and their cities had to form an areawide agency to develop the functional and comprehensive plans if they wished to continue receiving federal aid for their capital construction projects. The Demonstration Cities and Metropolitan Development Act of 1966 and the Intergovernmental Cooperation Act of 1968 carried the requirement for regional conformity one step further: they declared that an areawide planning agency would have the authority to review and comment on local applications before submission to the federal departments for approval. These requirements prompted quick action. New organizations— councils of governments—were quickly formed to undertake areawide planning (assisted by federal planning grants) and grant application reviews. Between 1968, when the review requirement was passed, and 1969, the number of councils increased from 100 to 175; now the number is well over 300.[19] While councils are heavily subsidized by federal grants, especially for planning, member cities and counties are required to pay dues—another commitment for local budgets.

In addition to planning requirements, federal grants demand conformance with civil rights and minimum wage laws; local employees working on federally funded programs are covered by the Hatch Act which outlaws participation in partisan politics.

Playing the Federal "Grantsmanship" Game

Local officials complain frequently about the impact of

185

federal money on local affairs. There are too many programs; the application process is too long and complicated; bureaucrats in Washington, the state capital and the county have too much power; local objectives have to be subordinated to the state and the national. "You just have to admit," says Jackson County, Missouri executive George E. Lehr, "the feds have proven beyond a shadow of a doubt that they can deliver services more inefficiently than any other level of government."[20] However, county officials generally endorse the grant system—they need the money, and they realize the concept is too well-entrenched to be dismantled for another method. Consequently, they have taken steps to keep on top of it. Some county commissioners take the direct approach—contacting their senators and representatives. A top aide to the mayor-president of Baton Rouge-East Baton Rouge Parish explained: "When applications bounce back and forth between us and them (sic) five or six times, in a state of utter futility, I ask the mayor to call Washington and get in touch with people up there and finally get the job done."[21] The mayor happens, incidentally, to be a childhood friend of Senator Russell B. Long, Chairman of the Senate Finance Committee.

Other county governing boards have become expert at the game of federal "grantsmanship," elevating it to professional status. Nearly 400 counties have hired a federal aid coordinator (or community development coordinator) whose job is to oversee the local grant process. In many counties, the governing boards have established a new office or department, with the coordinator responsible directly to it. Other counties have assigned the responsibility to existing departments; to the planning commission in Genesee County, Michigan; to the public works department in Tarrant County, Texas; and to the budget office in Mesa County, California. Coordinators have one job—bring in more federal money. Done well, the assignment can assume herculean proportions as testified to by the following list of essential duties:[22]

advise commissioners in preparing annual operating and capital budgets

inform county commissioners about congressional and state legislative action on grant programs

monitor actions of federal and state agencies which administer the programs, and review and comment on proposed administrative regulations

package various grants, such as employee training programs to ensure that they dovetail, locally

maintain liaison with other public and semi-public agencies receiving federal assistance in the area.

Coordinators not only make sense out of the jumble of over 1000 federal grant programs, they also can curtail the excessive independence of appointed department heads, enabling the elected officials to control their governments more effectively. Better control results especially where governing board members refuse to sign an application without approval of the coordinator, and notify department heads not to prepare applications without the coordinator's preliminary okay.

Seven counties have set up offices in Washington for on-the-spot coverage of the federal government. Because of the increasing competition for federal funds, the attempts of the Nixon administration to reorganize the grant-in-aid system, and the growth and complexity of the federal bureaucracy, these counties want direct influence on federal laws and policies. Counties without a Washington representative can rely on the National Association of Counties (NACO) to keep track of the Washington scene. NACO has a membership of over 800 counties, representing 60 percent of the nation's population.[23] The association seeks to influence federal grants through the legislative process and by working with the federal bureaucracy. One of its great strengths is the ties its membership has with representatives and senators. Some individuals, for example, are personal friends of the chairmen of the House Appropriations Committee, the Senate Finance Committee, and the House Rules Committee. The importance of these contacts was exemplified recently by the authorization of funds for sewer and water facilities. The grant program called for federal payment of up to 50 percent of the construction costs for new sewer and water lines, most of them being built in suburban or rapidly urbanizing counties. In the 91st Congress, NACO lobbyists were instrumental in raising the authorization from $100 million to $1 billion in a single year, despite opposition from the President and Republican members of Congress.[24]

NACO's efforts to raise money for counties goes beyond the enactment of laws. The association carefully oversees the federal administration of grant programs. In 1970 when the Department of Housing and Urban Development was extremely dilatory in approving grants for water and sewer facilities, NACO managed to obtain a computer printout which showed an application backlog of $2.5 billion, at a time when HUD's official backlog was only $500 million. The statistics were broken down by congressional district, and the NACO staff made sure that each congressman was informed.[25] The logjam quickly disappeared. More recently, NACO was instrumental in achieving equal treatment for counties and cities under the 1973 Comprehensive Employment and Training Act, while the draft legislation differentiated between the two—to the county's detriment.

NACO concentrates on six major fields: public works, health and welfare, law enforcement, manpower training, airport development and mass transit. Commissioners and executives of member counties are organized into corresponding steering committees, according to the member's interests or contacts in the functional area. The lobbying effort is supported by research on county government issues by the New County Center, devoted to studying and promoting county government reforms, and by project work under federal grants in areas of interest to counties, such as developing a series of manuals on solid waste disposal, outdoor recreation and pollution control. Although NACO was organized in 1937, it did not become a powerful influence in Washington until its first and still serving executive director, Bernard F. Hillenbrand, was hired twenty years later. NACO is headed by a president elected for a one-year term, four vice presidents and a 48-member board of directors. To date the presidency has rotated among representatives of rural and urban counties.

Efforts to Reform the Grants System

A movement toward simplification of the grants system began in the mid-1960s, just at the time when a host of new programs were being enacted. Studies were undertaken by the Bureau of the Budget, the Advisory Commission on Intergovernmental Relations, and the Senate Subcommittee on Intergovernmental Relations. The result has been creation of a coordinating system which is nearly as complex as the grants system itself, plus some new approaches to distributing funds.

Emphasis on coordination was reflected in the Model Cities program, for example, designed to coordinate federal resources to combat all problems in one section of a city or a county; the Economic Opportunity program designed to combine all federal resources for eliminating poverty; and the economic development programs to upgrade rural areas. By 1967 the number of local coordinating mechanisms developed in response to the federal efforts was getting out of hand—there were community action agencies, city demonstration agencies, resource conservation and development projects, and on and on.

In 1968 a new administration brought a different philosophy of intergovernmental relations and a continued interest in simplifying the grant-in-aid system. President Nixon's New Federalism was a proposal to revamp the meth-

189

ods of federal distribution to states and localities. The intent was to give more local discretion in the use of monies and increase the control of local elected officials by simplifying the application process and by combining grant programs.

A major part of the New Federalism was enacted by the State and Local Fiscal Assistance Act of 1972, commonly known as the general revenue sharing law. In a complete reversal of the categorical grant system, it allocates roughly $6 billion per year to state and local governments for five years, with virtually no strings attached. Essentially the funds can be spent on projects which local, not national, officials designate as high priority.

County officials have welcomed revenue sharing as an increase in their budgets for programs of high priority. For many small counties it will be a first experience with federal grants. For some large counties, it will account for a significant portion of the budget—17 percent in New Castle County, Delaware, 15 percent in Columbus-Muscogee County, Georgia, and 12 percent in St. Louis County, Missouri.[26]

After one year of revenue sharing a Georgia county commissioner remarked, "This program, as was promised, has allowed local officials and their citizens to consider, set and meet local priorities without the intrusion from above that is present in other federal assistance programs."[27] A similar enthusiasm from his fellow commissioners and county executives also stems from the fact that revenue sharing funds will make increases in property and other taxes unnecessary and, in a few cases, allow for reductions in tax rates. Although revenue sharing has "cut the strings," county officials have allocated their funds with an eye, not only to local needs, but to federal policies as well. Generally, county commissioners have used their initial revenue sharing payments for capital improvements or projects not requiring a long-term financial commitment. For example, Muscogee County, Georgia spent $50,000 sprucing up its recreation centers. Why? Because the federal revenue sharing program expires in 1976, and who can predict the future in politics?[28]

All is not favorable, however. About the time revenue sharing went into effect, the federal government began to cut back funds in other grant programs—housing and urban development, sewer and water projects, community action programs and health services, among many others. Facing the loss of income for ongoing programs, county officials were forced to use general revenue sharing funds to make up the difference. The reaction of the mayor of Kaui County, Hawaii, expressed the feelings of many of his colleagues.

> If, as a result of general revenue sharing, other federal programs were to be eliminated or reduced, in the future only greater problems can be anticipated . . . a possible reduction in federal grant monies would be totally unsatisfactory and would force the county to disapprove the concept of general revenue sharing.[29]

The Nixon administration has proposed to supplement general revenue sharing with special revenue sharing funds in six functional areas: urban and rural community development, law enforcement, transportation, education and manpower. Special revenue sharing proposals are designed to consolidate the multitude of grants for related activities, such as the separate Labor Department training programs, and to allow counties, states and cities to use a large sum of money for any of a variety of local needs within a specific functional area.

To date, federal aid for law enforcement, manpower and rural development is administered according to New Federalism principles. The approach has been used for law enforcement since 1968 (the Safe Streets Act was passed during the Johnson administration). The Law Enforcement Assistance Administration gives money to states which have submitted acceptable plans for upgrading law enforcement and judicial systems; the states develop their own priorities for allocating the money to counties and cities. Manpower reforms became law with the enactment of the Comprehensive Employment and Training Act of 1973; it replaces hundreds of grant programs with a single allocation of money to states and specified cities and counties. Special revenue sharing for rural areas is embodied in the Rural Development Act of 1972. However, this program has not been funded fully, and more emphasis has been placed on its provision to loan money to governments in rural areas rather than to award non-repayable grants.

It is too early to predict whether the other special revenue sharing proposals will be enacted or how well the recent reforms will work. Furthermore, no one predicts a complete demise of categorical grants. Clearly the existing system of intergovernmental relations would be altered drastically. County officials would have freer rein to use federal money for locally determined purposes. However, there are several opponents who want control to remain at the national level, including members of Congress, who presently determine the allocation of monies through categorical grant programs. They have the power to scrutinize spending activity and often intervene to obtain grants for their constituent counties and cities. Under the special revenue sharing system, congressmen would have little control over who receives the funds or how they are spent. In effect, they would be giving state and local officials greater power to finance constituent-pleasing services. As former HEW Secretary Wilbur Cohen observed, "When congressmen meet in executive session to discuss relaxing the restrictions on categorical grants, someone always says, 'Joe, do you know who is going to run against you in two, four, six years? Maybe the governor or a mayor!' "[30]

Special interest groups also prefer categorical grants because some are designed especially for them, as opposed to the special revenue sharing grants which give local officials more discretion. Some officials find it advantageous to be "forced" to spend money on politically dangerous projects. The mayor of New Orleans pointed out that the interests of the black community probably would not have been taken into account were it not for federal categorical grants, as blacks have not been represented on the city council.[31]

Federal ófficials who administer grant programs also prefer continuation of the present system, under which they have final authority to approve and reject applications. They like dealing with their professional colleagues at the state and local levels, which makes the shift in policy making from appointed to elected officials unattractive.

The Nixon administration has continued to pursue greater authority for elected state and local officials. By executive order the President established common boundaries for all regional offices of federal agencies and established regional councils consisting of field office representatives of various federal departments and agencies. This is to enable county officials to take their grants problems to one nearby office for help, at least theoretically. The regional council members help to coordinate grants, and are supposed to give final approval on applications as well. However, the plan has not been implemented fully. Some departments, such as HUD and the Department of Labor, have delegated decision making to field officers, but HEW, the department dispensing most federal assistance, retains full control at the top.

Two experiments in simplifying grants are being conducted. One, under test in a few localities, allows the jurisdiction to identify community needs and goals, preparing only one application for assistance. Federal officers do the rest, which means tracking down the appropriate categorical grants, determining the money available, and ensuring that it is channeled to the community. The second experiment, being tested in twenty cities, is designed to keep mayors abreast of the grants in their community. Known as the Chief Executive Review and Comment, it authorizes mayors to review and comment on all grant applications affecting their cities, including those submitted by counties, neighboring cities, and semipublic and private groups. This experiment poses serious problems for counties; if implemented nationwide, it would give city officials some direct control over county policies. The problem is especially acute in San Jose, California, one of the pilot cities. The mayor needed more information about the federal money coming into his city because "city agencies were applying right and left for money and the mayor's office never knew what the extent of the city's matching commitments were. And, of course, we never had the chance to weigh the individual commitments to any kind of needs assessment."[32] However, the executive of Santa Clara County, which includes San Jose, sees no basis for allowing the mayor to pass judgment on the county's grants. After all, the county budget is five times greater than the city's; the county offers a far more complete line of services and receives far more federal money. Wisely, the mayor has limited his review to a comprehensive list of grants received by the city alone.

Where to from Here?

The general goals of the Nixon administration are clear, but the ultimate extent of their realization is less certain. Relationships among federal, state and local officials, and the balance of power among them, remain unsettled. In a variety of areas, county officials look to the federal government for both money and leadership. On the other hand, the federal government has no choice but to rely on state and local officials to carry out national objectives in their areas. Such mutual dependence breeds conflict as well as cooperation, but it is a partnership in which each level of government plans its role in serving the same constituents. These respective roles probably will continue to shift. The degree of authority over specific functions, such as welfare, seems likely to be further modified.

Counties have become partners in the intergovernmental system. However, there is room for them to press for more complete status, especially as the emphasis on regional and

194

rural government continues to intensify. Their role in the administration and implementation of services is unquestioned, but there is great need for counties to assert themselves in the decisions about local priorities and the designing of local policies.

Notes

1. Banfield, Edward C. and James Q. Wilson, *City Politics,* (New York: Vintage Books, 1963), p. 73.

2. Abrams, Charles, *The City Is the Frontier* (New York: Harper Colophon Books, 1965), p. 213.

3. *Special Analysis N of the United States Budget for Fiscal Year 1975.* (Washington, D.C.: U.S. Government Printing Office, 1974), p. 210.

4. *Ibid.*

5. *Ibid.*

6. "A Guide to Grantsmanship for County Officials" (Washington, D.C.: National Association of Counties, 1973), preface.

7. Shaskan, Carol, "Status of Selected Categorical Grant Programs, December 1, 1973" (Washington, D.C.: National Association of Counties).

8. "A Guide to Grantsmanship," p. 1-3.

9. *Ibid.*

10. *The National Journal,* vol. 5, no. 3, p. 87.

11. *Ibid.*

12. *Ibid.,* p. 83.

13. Sundquist, James L. with David W. Davis, *Making Federalism Work* (Washington, D.C.: The Brookings Institution, 1969), p. 4.

14. *The National Journal,* vol. 5, no. 7, p. 219.

15. *Ibid.*

16. Advisory Commission on Intergovernmental Relations, *Fiscal Balance in the American Federal System,* vol. 1

(Washington, D.C.: U.S. Government Printing Office, 1967), p. 190.

17. *Ibid.*, p. 153.

18. *Ibid.*, p. 178.

19. Mogulof, Melvin B., *Governing Metropolitan Areas,* (Washington, D.C.: The Urban Institute, 1971), p. 1.

20. *The National Journal,* vol. 5, no. 7, p. 21.

21. *Ibid.*, vol. 5, no. 3, p. 83.

22. "A Guide to Grantsmanship for County Officials."

23. *The National Journal,* vol. 3, no. 22.

24. *Ibid.*

25. *Ibid.*

26. *County News,* vol. 5, no. 42, November 2, 1973.

27. *Ibid.*, vol. 5, no. 40, October 19, 1973.

28. *Ibid.*, vol. 5, no. 41, October 26, 1973.

29. *Ibid.*, vol. 5, no. 40, October 19, 1973.

30. *The National Journal,* vol. 4, no. 51, p. 1927.

31. *Ibid.*

32. *Ibid.*

8.   Counties and the Future of America

A form of government older than America itself, counties historically have been in the background. In varying degrees, however, almost all counties have become more responsive to the contemporary needs of their citizens. Now, some political scientists and practical politicians feel that counties may be the local government of the future. For this to be true, counties must meet several challenges. Can they work effectively with neighboring cities and counties to address urban problems? Will they attain the authority and effectiveness needed to assume a meaningful role as regional governments? Can rural counties develop a professionalism sufficient to fuel the impetus to what seems to be a revitalization of rural America? Can counties, urban and rural, sustain the financial burden from the ever increasing demand for public services?

The following interview gives one expert's answers. Bernard F. Hillenbrand has been executive director of the National Association of Counties since 1957. He is a national spokesman, working with county officials to develop modern and effective local government.

An Interview with Bernard F. Hillenbrand

Mrs. Torrence: Today about fifty-eight million

197

Americans live in the suburbs. Most of these citizens seem to be very proud of their small town governments and they identify very closely with them. Twenty-five years from now, do you think these citizens will look first to city hall or to the county courthouse for political leadership and for public services?

Mr. Hillenbrand: Well, up until the energy crisis I would have said they very definitely would be looking toward the county courthouse. With the energy crisis, I'm not quite as sure. . . . A lot depends on how prolonged the energy crisis is and how severe it is. I note, for example, a spate of stories on behalf of builders, that they're going to start building now in the central cities rather than in the suburbs.

Item: The planning department of Erie County, which is Buffalo, New York, already has their planning department completely redoing their general land use plan to plan all development around the mass transit system. So these could be factors that could profoundly influence the future growth of the county.

Other than this, however, the trend overwhelmingly is toward much wider use of the county than in the past. I think it's very important to keep in mind that those same central cities, that same city hall is, generally speaking, in the county. The people who live in that central city are still citizens of the county, they vote for the county officials, they pay taxes to the county and they are served by their county. So those factors are not likely to change.

Q: What do you see as the future of the central city? Will county officials help shape that future?

A: I look for the central city, barring a catastrophe because of the energy crisis, I look for the central city to be an urban service district within the county to provide such things as intense police protection, artificial street lighting, curbs and gutters, trash collection, and that type of thing, and be like a giant multipurpose special service district, with the county itself providing basic governmental services, i.e., the

198

administration of justice, all the things to do with humans—mental health, juvenile delinquency control, hospital, welfare, education, libraries, community colleges, these things that are fantastically expensive and that benefit everybody in the county, whether they live on a farm, or a suburban area or the central city. In other words, I see that the real basic government of the future will be the county and that the city will be increasingly a special service district to provide intensive urban services for a relatively smaller geographic area.

Q: Does this imply a political reorganization of the city and the county?

A: I think that in many cases it will. We certainly do not have a huge progress report on city/county consolidations, and that may not be the direction we go. I think it will be more in terms of keeping the same structures we have now, but reallocating the functions.

Item: Counties, for example, are increasingly the agency to provide basic water supply and sewage treatment, even though the city might be an agent of the county in the sense of selling the water or charging a fee for the collection of sewage.

Item: The city police would provide street patrols and so on, but the county would have the crime laboratory, would have the record keeping, would probably have the public works garage and buy equipment, would have control of the radio system. This type of thing. I look for the future to be more a reallocation of functions within the existing political framework.

Q: Do you think this reallocation will take place through joint cooperation of the city and county? What role will the state play in this process?

A: Well, the state is a relative newcomer, strangely enough, to urban affairs, but the state has shown incredible change of direction in the past five to eight years.

You find the states now intervening increasingly in the question of sub-districting. They are intervening increasingly

199

in the area of mass transit, beginning to get more involved in housing and some of these other subjects. I think again, throwing in the uncertainty of the energy crisis, it's certain that the state is going to have an increasing leadership role in emerging problems like land use control, energy and other functions, so we look for a much wider role for the states, and I might also add that the National Association of Counties has always preferred a wider role for the states in contrast to some of the city organizations, who have been in favor of more direct relationships between the federal government and the localities.

Q: All these programs that you envision for counties, such as social programs and sewage disposal and so forth, will be quite expensive. Where are counties going to find the money to support them?

A: Well part of the money, frankly, is going to have to come from the federal government, in the sense that the principal source of income at the county level is the property tax, and the property tax simply is not lucrative enough or flexible enough to provide basic things like the cost of caring for a mentally ill child, which can run in any single year to many thousands of dollars and has no relationship to the property tax we collect from the parents of that mentally ill child. We've got some precedents established now on the national level.

Item: We have passed the general revenue sharing law which is a method of harnessing the federal income tax, which is geared to ability to pay, and taking the proceeds of that and sharing it with the states, cities, and counties.

Item: We have now done this same thing in manpower legislation, where we have reduced the number of sponsors, prime sponsors in manpower, from thousands and thousands to a hundred and sixty cities and two hundred and seventy counties. These prime sponsors then will be receiving funds on a formula basis, which takes into account need, population,

200

poverty and other factors, and so this is another example of the kinds of legislation and administrative techniques we think will be used in the future to provide the counties with the type of funds they need to respond to these human problems.

Q: We've been talking so far about urban counties, but about two thousand counties are rural. What will be their fate in the next twenty-five years?

A: Again we have an uncertainty here. In the very, very recent past, i.e., the spring of 1973 and beyond, there has been a very, very sharp increase in the price of food. If this trend continues, and if American farmers are going to have equity with other aspects of American economic life, you could find a very profound change in rural America. I, for one, am strongly of the opinion that the demand for food is now world-wide, and that the United States' future, a large part of it economically, will depend upon providing food for the world. If this is the case, we believe that the economic situation in the rural areas for the first time in a couple of hundred years will be turned about, and that there will be an increasing flow of money into these communities. This will be particularly the case if more and more of the food processing is done in rural areas and doesn't get concentrated in central cities.

By that I mean the processing of flour and vegetables and other types of food and preparing for freezing and so on. If these kinds of activities are kept in the rural areas, and I suspect they may be, then rural counties will have a new birth of economic life and a new economic base. Our reading of recent trends where all the people, or such large numbers of people left the rural areas is that they didn't leave the rural areas because they were escaping something, it's because they had no real economic base and no economic future, and I think that'll change.

There's still another factor. Many of the areas which have been losing population, i.e., Appalachia and the regions around southern Illinois and some of the western areas, these are mining communities, where they have mined coal and other minerals, and I suspect that there will also be a very great revival in these areas of economic interest. I think it would very well behoove the United States to be sure, if we go now into a massive new program of producing and processing coal to make gasoline and so on, that we are sure that the local communities are given a share of that wealth in the form of extraction taxes and other kinds of taxation, so that they can make the rural areas of the United States as viable as the suburban areas.

Q: And how is this going to affect the leadership of county government?

A: I think that it will strengthen the leadership because if the counties, in the rural areas, have a greater economic base, I think they will be able to respond to the natural inclinations of the citizen which is to want the very best and the widest array of services. I look, for example, for a great improvement in the education system, more and bigger and better community colleges, better hospitals and medical care, and a whole host of services to rural areas, which are now lacking because there's no economic base.

Q: You have mentioned several attributes of counties. Are there any inherent weaknesses in this form of government?

A: The principal weakness at this moment is lack of a single official comparable to a president at the national level, a governor at the state level or a mayor at the municipal level. We do have a position at the county level in almost all counties called chairman of the board, but this position typically rotates every year, the person holding this position doesn't have any more authority or power than the other members of the county board, and he is not elected on any special basis to be head of the county like a mayor or a governor is. We see the trend in the future toward increasing the authority and building this position of chairman of the board into some type of executive.

202

This is our principal weakness of the county government level now—we are basically organized like a British parliament in the sense that each of the members of the county governing body is elected by districts and then they get together and among themselves select, in effect, a prime minister, and it's my opinion that this system has not worked as well as a strong executive position, i.e., a strong governor or a mayor or president. The county experience of multiple leadership is contrary to our experience in business. In the business world there's a president of the corporation or chairman of the board who has executive power greatly exceeding that of the individual board members.

To put it still another way, I think that what we need at the county level, what we need to overcome, is this multiple leadership problem, and the solution is to separate the legislative from the executive, and have either a strong elected executive and/or an elected executive and a professionally appointed manager. I think this is the trend in the recent past.

Item: In the state of New York ninety percent of the people now live in counties that have an elected county executive, and in almost every one of those cases the elected county executive position, comparable to that of a mayor, also has a professionally trained administrative officer comparable to a county manager.

Q: Today many state constitutions and laws have prevented counties from reorganizing. Some of these are now being changed. By 1980, do you think that state legislators will have a different attitude toward counties and what do you think that attitude might be?

A: By 1980, indeed I would suspect much sooner than that, probably by 1976, during the Bicentennial, I suspect that almost all states will have legislation which we call home rule legislation, which will take the following forms. It will provide for an optional executive of some type, an appointed and/or elected executive. It will provide for a separation of powers in a sense that it will remove judicial, administrative and legislative powers from the same body. It'll be in keeping with the division of powers in the rest of the American government structure.

I suspect that this same state enabling legislation will allow for the appointment of certain key department heads at the local government level, rather than their election. I think these are some of the basic changes that will be made, and in addition to this, I think that by 1976 you will find increasingly that counties will have the power to change their administrative structure by local regulation, and will have additional powers, powers of selective taxation within broad guidelines established by the state, and that there will be other items of reform that will be extended at the county government level that were extended to cities about twenty-five or thirty years ago. The push for all this will come from the fact that the counties are becoming very large, important units of government.

Item: I worked for Onondaga County in the city of Syracuse in 1957, and at that time the city budget was much larger than the county's. This year the city budget is much smaller than the county's. This dramatic reversal of relative importance and costliness of county government is due to the great expansion of the role of county government and I think that this is more or less typical throughout the United States.

Q: The future of counties will also be shaped by the policies of the federal government. We alluded to some of these earlier. What assignments do you think the federal government would like to see counties carry out?

A: Well starting with the most recent and working back. The most recent is the proposal by the administration to create on a standby basis, county-wide rationing control boards, apparently paralleling the ones that we used to have in drafts, local citizen boards. There would be one in every county and some counties will have more than one. Again moving backward from today, manpower legislation just passed by

204

the federal government and signed by the President of the United States allows two-hundred and seventy counties to be prime sponsors under manpower. I might add that the counties were not even involved in manpower up until two or three years ago. They now act as administrative units for what is called the public employment program, or PEP program, and they have done a really outstanding job. That caused the Congress and the President to advocate a wider role for them in the area of manpower.

Still another case in point of the expansion of counties is general revenue sharing. It's probably not clearly understood by the citizens, but some forty-eight percent of all the money that goes to cities and counties goes to the counties, almost half of it. The formulas are so geared that as we progress (since they're based upon population and revenue effort and so on) the county share is almost certain to exceed that of the cities. It's one more indication of the volume of activity and new importance of counties.

If we go further into the future, the administration has proposed exactly the same kind of a role for counties in housing, community development and urban renewal. It's been proposed in the area of education and many other areas, and we believe that this will be the trend of the future, a much wider use of county government as a viable unit of local government, and I might add that I believe this is going to be the case regardless of whether we have a Democrat or a Republican administration at the national level.

Q: So far we've been talking about the things that counties will do for their constituents, but citizens also have various obligations to their government. What do you think county officials expect from their constituents?

A: I think the very first thing that the counties would like to have is some understanding among the local citizens of what the functions are of the county. If you look at the principal services now provided by the counties, they are hidden from the view of the general public, i.e., we run the jails, and the average citizen isn't in the jail. We run the courts and the average citizen does not go to court every day. We run the welfare program, but most of the citizens do not receive funds under that, so they don't understand what the county is doing in that area. We run hospitals, but again the citizen doesn't always understand that we're doing that. Not every citizen is in the hospital every year.

By contrast, if you see the city government level, they typically do things that have high visibility, i.e., they have policemen, firemen and trash collectors. These are on the street all the time and the citizen is constantly aware of what a city is providing, but he does not really understand what the county provides, particularly since the kinds of services the county provides are extremely costly and concern only relatively small numbers of people. They are in the human services area. The first thing the counties would really like to have is better understanding from the citizen of what a county is all about.

And I might add that this would also be helpful if the press understood it. We constantly hear the press saying well, the President has proposed that the governors and the mayors do so and so, and the actual reality is that he's proposing that the governors, mayors and the county officials do something, so we are constantly faced with this dilemma of the citizen not understanding what a county is all about, and again this goes back to the fact that we're not properly organized in terms of making that come about.

For example, almost everybody in the United States knows that the Mayor of Los Angeles City is Tom Bradley, and the city has about two and a half million people. But there wouldn't be a half a dozen people in the United States that would know that the chairman of the board of that county, which has seven million people, and provides an infinitely vaster array of services and spends much more money, that the chairman of that board is Kenny Hahn. This is the kind of a dilemma that we have in our multiple leadership counties. It isn't that the counties are poorly administered under the committee system. It is that the citizen doesn't understand because there is no contest for the chief elected office and there's no way to focus public attention on the office with the multiple leadership situation.

Summing Up

Offering basic public services regionwide, helping stimulate rural areas, taking on new assignments—community colleges, dental care, mental health, housing, mass transit, perhaps rationing gasoline and testing new types of fuel. Unquestionably, this is a full agenda.

How well counties respond—their ability to define issues, develop plans of action, and then follow through—depends on the caliber of their leadership. But the ability to attract leaders depends, in part, on how effective counties have been in the past, as well as the potential rewards of holding a time-consuming office with burdensome responsibilities. One of the greatest rewards is public recognition—the acknowledgement by the average citizen that being at the helm of a county government is a substantive and essential task. Many persons are reluctant to hold public office at any level, national, state or local, but potential leaders are encouraged by opportunities for high visibility and high public esteem.

This reward is absent in too many counties. As Robert C. Wood, former Secretary of HUD and now president of the University of Massachusetts observed, "Ever since James Bryce (author of *American Commonwealth* in 1895) called the counties the 'dark continent of American politics,' they have been associated in the public mind with images of sloth and ineptitude."[1] Some counties still have to shake the image of the courthouse gang behind closed doors making decisions in smoke filled rooms.

As a result too many citizens have disregarded counties

without taking an objective look. On the other hand, too many county officials have allowed the myth to continue. They have done a poor job of developing a more representative public image. Admittedly the county courthouse remains, but one look at the glittering office buildings of Fairfax County, Virginia, or of Santa Clara County, California, dispels the notion that the old structure represents what is going on in counties today. However, developing a better image has not been an easy task, hindered as it has been by the absence of a single officeholder who speaks with authority for the entire county. This is one reason cities have the edge over counties in the public eye. As one California county official put it,

> We just don't have the glitter and the political pizzaz that a mayor does. Even if a mayor is not strong, people identify with him as the chief executive. More important for the counties, a weak mayor with largely ceremonial functions can come to Washington, and he still is regarded by federal officials as the chief executive for all important functions, even though that may not be true.[2]

For years reform-minded citizens, scholars, and politicians have debated the impact of governmental structure on governmental performance. Some have claimed that the formal distribution of power is less important than the informal roles assumed by individual politicians, while others have claimed that governments must be organized properly if they are to function properly. The debates can continue, but it is hard to discount the value of having one official authorized to represent the county and all of its constituents.

Within the last twenty years, there has been a pronounced movement toward the executive type of county government. Thirty counties have switched to this form of government since 1960 and the trend is expected to continue. Of course, executives cannot govern counties by themselves; they must have aggressive council members and qualified administrative personnel. Nevertheless, the future status of county government, its impact on the lives of millions of Americans, and its role in our federal system of government will be shaped by those elected to lead it and the confidence of the citizens in their ability to govern.

Notes

1. *The National Journal,* vol. 3, no. 22, p. 1133.
2. *Ibid.*

Appendix

What Is a County?

Not even the experts (the U.S. Bureau of the Census, the Advisory Commission on Intergovernmental Relations - ACIR - and the National Association of Counties - NACO) agree on what a county is and how many there are.

The ACIR maintains there are 3146 county-type areas falling into two categories:

those having their own constituency and clearly defined political and geographic boundaries;
those lacking an independently organized county government.

Most counties fall in the first category but the ACIR and the Census Bureau disagree over whether the exact number is 3049 (ACIR) or 3045 (Census Bureau) because they treat Alaskan boroughs and consolidated city-counties differently. The ACIR counts all nine Alaskan boroughs; the Census Bureau counts only four of them.

The remaining 100 or so county-type areas do not have an independent government and are split into four groups:

city-counties where the governing body acts primarily as a city. There are five: San Francisco, Denver, Honolulu,

Juneau, and Nashville. (The ACIR calls the latter a city-county; the Census Bureau calls it a metropolitan government and puts it in a separate category.)

areas with county officers but no distinct government or with county officers serving as city, township, parish or state officials as well. There are four, according to the ACIR and the Census Bureau: New Orleans and Orleans Parish, Baton Rouge and East Baton Rouge Parish; Nantucket city and county and Boston and Suffolk County, Massachusetts; New York City and its five boroughs; and Philadelphia City and County.

cities located outside of counties which administer some functions performed elsewhere by counties. There are 45: Washington, D.C.; Baltimore City; St. Louis City; four consolidated city-county governments (Jacksonville-Duval County, Florida; Columbus-Muscogee County, Georgia; Indianapolis-Marion County, Indiana; Carson City-Ormsby County, Nevada); and 35 cities in Virginia—Virginia cities may secede from their county upon incorporation.

areas designated counties but which have no government. Sixteen of these are found in Connecticut, Rhode Island, and South Dakota, and only exist for election and judicial purposes; the remaining 19 are in Alaska and are census divisions.

The National Association of Counties maintains that there are 3106 counties, including consolidated city-counties and some traditionally regarded as cities (such as New York).

Title of Governing Boards by State

Alabama	Board of Commissioners or Board of Revenue
Alaska	Borough Assembly
Arizona	Board of Supervisors
Arkansas	Quorum or Levying Court Chaired by County Judge
California	Board of Supervisors
Colorado	Board of County Commissioners*
Connecticut	No County Governing Board
Delaware	Levy Court in Kent and Sussex Counties
Florida	Board of County Commissioners*
Georgia	Board of Commissioners
Hawaii	Borough Assembly
Idaho	Board of County Commissioners*
Illinois	Board of Supervisors or Board of Commissioners
Indiana	Board of County Commissioners*
Iowa	County Board of Supervisors
Kansas	Board of County Commissioners*
Kentucky	Fiscal Court Chaired by County Judge and County Commissioner
Louisiana	Police Jury, Parish Council and Commission Council
Maine	Board of County Commissioners*
Maryland	Board of County Commissioners (called county council in six home rule counties)
Massachusetts	Board of County Commissioners*
Michigan	Board of Commissioners
Minnesota	County Board of Commissioners
Mississippi	County Board of Supervisors
Missouri	County Court
Montana	County Board of Commissioners

213

Nebraska	Board of Commissioners*
Nevada	Board of County Commissioners*
New Hampshire	Board of Commissioners
New Jersey	Board of Chosen Freeholders
New Mexico[1]	County Board of Commissioners*
New York	Board of County Legislators, Supervisors or Representatives
North Carolina	Board of County Commissioners*
North Dakota	County Board of Commissioners*
Ohio	Board of County Commissioners*
Oklahoma	Board of County Commissioners
Oregon	County Court
Pennsylvania	Board of County Commissioners*
Rhode Island	No functional counties
South Carolina	Board of Commissioners
South Dakota	Board of Commissioners*
Tennessee	County Court, County Council
Texas	Commissioners Court
Utah	Board of County Commissioners*
Vermont	County Judge
Virginia	Board of Supervisors (except in Arlington in which title is County Board)
Washington	Board of County Commissioners*
West Virginia	County Court
Wisconsin	Board of Supervisors
Wyoming[2]	County Board of Commissioners*

*Counties are divided into classes by population.

1–Nine classes of county based on population and assessed valuation.

2–Three classes of county based on assessed valuation.

Source: U.S. Department of Commerce, Bureau of Census, "Governing Boards of County Governments: 1965" (United States Government Printing Office: 1965), p. 3-4.

Distribution of Counties by Population

Population Category	Number of Counties
1,000,001–9,999,999	18*
500,001–1,000,000	50
250,001– 500,000	73*
100,001– 250,000	185
75,001– 100,000	118
50,001– 75,000	208
25,001– 50,000	566*
25,000 & under	1846

*These figures do not include areas having certain types of county offices, but each as part of another government (city, township, state). Those not included are: New York: Bronx, Kings, New York, Queens, Richmond; Pennsylvania: County of Philadelphia.

Source: population statistics from the U.S. Bureau of the Census, U.S. Census of Population: 1970, Final Report PC(1) A1, 1971. Figures prepared by National Association of Counties, 1972.

CHARTER COUNTIES

STATE County	Population 1970 Census	Form of Charter	Size of Legislative Body	Year of Charter Adoption
ALASKA				
Greater City of Sitka	6,109	Council – Elected Executive	7	1971
Juneau/Greater Juneau Borough	13,556	Council – Administration	9	1970
CALIFORNIA				
Alameda	1,073,184	Commission (Council)–Administrator	5	1926
Butte	101,969	Commission (Council)–Administrator	5	1917
Fresno	413,053	Commission (Council)–Administrator	5	1933
Los Angeles	7,032,075	Commission (Council)–Administrator	5	1912
Sacramento	631,498	Commission (Council)–Administrator	5	1933
San Bernardino	684,072	Commission (Council)–Administrator	5	1912
San Diego	1,357,854	Commission (Council)–Administrator	5	1933
San Francisco	715,674	Council – Elected Executive	11	1931
San Mateo	556,234	Commission (Council)–Administrator	5	1932
Santa Clara	1,064,714	Commission (Council)–Administrator	5	1950
Tehama	29,517	Commission (Council)–Administrator	5	1916
COLORADO				
Denver	514,678	Council – Elected Executive	9	1904

	Population	Form of Government	Council	Year
FLORIDA				
Dade	1,267,792	Commission (Council)–Administrator	9	1957
Jacksonville-Duval	528,865	Council – Elected Executive	19	1967
Sarasota	120,413	Commission (Council)–Administrator	5	1971
Volusia	169,487	Commission (Council)–Administrator	7	1970
GEORGIA				
Columbus-Muscogee	167,377	Council – Elected Executive	10	1970
HAWAII				
City and County of Honolulu	629,176	Council – Elected Executive	9	1959
Hawaii	63,468	Council – Elected Executive	9	1968
Kauai	29,761	Council – Elected Executive	7	1968
Maui	46,156	Council – Elected Executive	9	1968
KENTUCKY				
Lexington-Fayette	174,323	Council – Elected Executive	15	1972
Louisiana				
Baton Rouge-East Baton Rouge	285,167	Council – Elected Executive	11	1947
Jefferson	337,568	Council – Elected Executive	7	1956
MARYLAND				
Anne Arundel	297,539	Council – Elected Executive	7	1964
Baltimore	621,077	Council – Elected Executive	7	1956

Harford	115,378	Council – Elected Executive	7	1972
Howard	61,911	Council – Elected Executive	5	1968
Montgomery	522,809	Council – Elected Executive	7	1968
Prince George's	660,567	Council – Elected Executive	11	1970
Talbott	23,682	Council – Administrator	5	1973
Wicomico	54,236	Commission (Council)–Administrator	5	1964

MISSOURI

Jackson	654,558	Council – Elected Executive	15	1970
St. Louis	951,353	Council – Elected Executive	7	1968

NEW MEXICO

Los Alamos	15,198	Commission (Council)–Administrator	7	1968

NEW YORK

Albany	286,742	Council – Elected Executive	39	1973
Broome	221,815	Council – Elected Executive	19	1968
Chautauqua	147,305	Council – Elected Executive	25	1973
Chemung	101,537	Council – Elected Executive	16	1973
Dutchess	222,295	Council – Elected Executive	37	1967
Erie	1,113,491	Council – Elected Executive	20	1959
Herkimer	67,440	Commission	17	1966
Monroe	711,917	Commission (Council)–Administrator	29	1965
Nassau	1,422,905	Council – Elected Executive	6	1938
Oneida	273,037	Council – Elected Executive	37	1961
Onondaga	472,185	Council – Elected Executive	24	1961

	Population	Form of Government		Year
Orange	220,558	Council – Elected Executive	21	1968
Rensselaer	152,510	Council – Elected Executive	21	1972
Schenectady	100,979	Commission (Council)–Administrator	15	1965
Suffolk	1,116,672	Council – Elected Executive	18	1958
Tompkins	79,879	Commission (Council)–Administrator	16	1969
Westchester	891,409	Council – Elected Executive	17	1937
OREGON				
Benton	53,776	Commission	3	1972
Hood River	13,187	Commission (Council)–Administrator	5	1964
Lane	213,358	Commission	3	1962
Multnomah	556,667	Council – Elected Executive	5	1966
Washington	157,920	Commission (Council)–Administrator	5	1962
TENNESSEE				
Nashville-Davidson	448,003	Council – Elected Executive	40	1962
WASHINGTON				
King	1,156,633	Council – Elected Executive	9	1968

Single County Standard
Metropolitan Statistical Areas
(SMSA)

As of June 1972 there are 267 Standard Metropolitan Statistical Areas (single and multi-county).[1] The 127 Single County SMSA's reported here do not include the four municipos of Puerto Rico that are designated by the Bureau of the Census and OMB as being SMSAs.

The potential of the Single County SMSA to provide the nucleus for areawide government based on its population density, governmental structure and service delivery systems has been studied recently by the Advisory Commission on Intergovernmental Relations.

Alaska	Anchorage	Monterey
Alabama	Etowah	Orange
	Tuscaloosa	San Diego
Arizona	Maricopa	Santa Clara
	Pima	Santa Cruz
Arkansas	Jefferson	San Joaquin
California	Fresno	Sonoma
	Kern	Stanislaus
	Los Angeles	Ventura

[1]Each SMSA as of November 1971 includes at least one city with 50,000 population or more, or two cities with contiguous boundaries, constituting for general economic and social purposes a single community. The combined population of the two cities (often referred to as twin cities) has to be at least 50,000 with the population of the smaller being at least 15,000. When two or more adjacent counties meet this population criterion, and the cities are within 20 miles of each other (city limit to city limit) this constitutes a multi-county SMSA. If these criteria are met within one county, a single county SMSA is formed. Office of Management and Budget, *Standard Metropolitan Statistical Areas,* (Washington, D.C.: U.S. Government Printing Office. 1967), p. 1.

Colorado	El Paso		Calhoun
	Pueblo		Jackson
Florida	Alachua		Kalamazoo
	Brevard		Saginaw
	Broward		Washtenaw
	Dade	Minnesota	Olmsted
	Duval	Mississippi	Harrison
	Lee	Missouri	Boone
	Leon		Buchanan
	Palm Beach		Greene
	Polk	Montana	Cascade
	Sarasota		Yellowstone
	Volusia	Nebraska	Lancaster
Georgia	Chatham	Nevada	Clark
	Dougherty		Washoe
Hawaii	Honolulu	New Jersey	Atlantic
Idaho	Ada		Cumberland
Illinois	Champaign		Mercer
	McLean		Hudson
	Macon		Middlesex
	Sangamon		Monmouth
Indiana	Allen	New Mexico	Bernalillo
	Delaware	New York	Chemung
	Madison		Dutchess
	Tippecanoe		Nassau
Iowa	Black Hawk	North Carolina	Buncombe
	Dubuque		Cumberland
	Linn		Gaston
	Polk		Wake
Kansas	Shawnee	Ohio	Butler
Kentucky	Daviess		Clark
	Fayette		Lorain
Louisiana	Calcasiu		Richland
	East Baton		Stark
	Rouge	Oklahoma	Comanche
	Lafayette	Oregon	Lane
	Ouachita	Pennsylvania	Berks
	Rapides		Blair
Michigan	Bay		Erie

Counties with Elected Executives

Analysis by States

At present, 50 of America's counties have in their structure the position of elected county executive—one individual elected by the people and charged with the executive responsibility for the county. While the titles vary, each of the positions listed has been determined by the National Association of Counties, to meet the designation of "county executive."

The 50 executive counties have a total 1970 population of 27 million people. On a state-by-state basis the population breakdown for the county executives is:

State	Population Co. Exec. Counties	Number of County Executives
Alaska	164,056	7
California	715,674	1
Colorado	514,678	1
Delaware	385,856	1
Florida	1,796,657	2
Georgia	167,377	1
Hawaii	768,561	4
Illinois	5,492,369	1
Indiana	792,299	1
Kentucky	174,323	1
Louisiana	1,316,206	3
Maryland	3,215,040	7
Missouri	1,605,911	2
New York	6,106,877	9
Oregon	556,667	1
Tennessee	448,003	1
Washington	1,156,633	1
Wisconsin	1,751,866	5

Elected County Executives

Name	Year First Election Held	Year Office Established	Tern of Office (Years)
Greater Anchorage Area Borough, Alaska	1964	1964	3
North Slope Boroush Barrow Alaska	1972	1972	—
North Star Borough, Alaska	1963	1963	2
Haines Borough, Alaska	1968	1968	1
Kenai Peninsula Borough, Alaska	1963	1963	3
Ketchikan Gateway Borough, Alaska	1963	1963	3
Kodiak Island Borough, Alaska	1965	1963	2
City & County of San Francisco, California	1931	1931	4
City& County of Denver, Colorado	1904	1904	4
New Castle County, Delaware	1966	1965	4
Metropolitan Dade County, Florida	1958	1957	4
City of Jacksonville (Duval County), Florida	1967	1967	4
Columbus-Muscogee County, Georgia	1970	1970	4
Hawaii County, Hawaii	1969	1968	4

224

City & County of Honolulu, Hawaii	1908	1907	4
Kauai County, Hawaii	1968	1968	2
Maui County, Hawaii	1905	1905	2
Cook County, Illinois	1831	1831	4
Indianapolis-Marion County, Indiana	1971	1969	4
Lexington-Fayette County, Kentucky	1973	1972	4
Baton Rouge-East Baton Rouge Parish, Louisiana	1948	1947	4
Jefferson Parish, Louisiana	1958	1957	4
New Orleans, Louisiana	1954	1954	4
Anne Arundel County, Maryland	1965	1964	4
Harford County, Maryland	1957	1957	4
Baltimore County, Maryland	1957	1957	4
City of Baltimore, Maryland	1797	1797	4
Howard County, Maryland	1969	1968	4
Montgomery County, Maryland	1970	1968	4
Prince George's County, Maryland	1971	1970	4
Jackson County, Missouri	1973	1970	4
St. Louis County, Missouri	1950	1950	4
Broome County, New York	1970	1968	4
Dutchess County, New York	1967	1967	4
Erie County, New York	1959	1959	4
Nassau County, New York	1938	1938	3
Oneida County, New York	1962	1962	4
Onondaga County, New York	1962	1962	4
Orange County, New York	1969	1968	4
Rensselaer County, New York	1973	1972	4
Suffolk County, New York	1959	1958	4
Westchester County, New York	1938	1938	4
Multnomah County, Oregon	1965	1965	4
Metropolitan Government of Nashville-Davidson County, Tennessee	1963	1962	4
King County, Washington	1969	1968	4

225

Brown County, Wisconsin	1971	1970	4
Dane County, Wisconsin	1973	1972	4
Milwaukee County, Wisconsin	1960	1959	4
Outagamie County, Wisconsin	1971	1970	4
Winnebago County, Wisconsin	1973	1972	4

Notes:

1. Chautauqua, New York Elected Executive November 1974.
2. Albany, New York Elected Executive November 1974
3. Chemung, New York Elected Executive November 1974, but Board of Supervisors will appoint an Executive before leaving office December, 1973.

Ten Largest and Ten Smallest Counties

County	State	Population
County	*State*	*Population*
Los Angeles	California	7,032,075
Cook	Illinois	5,492,369
Wayne	Michigan	2,666,751
Harris	Texas	1,741,912
Cuyahoga	Ohio	1,721,300
Allegheny	Pennsylvania	1,605,016
Nassau	New York	1,422,905
Orange	California	1,420,386
Middlesex	Massachusetts	1,397,268
San Diego	California	1,357,854
Kennedy	Texas	678
Petroleum	Montana	675
Daggett	Utah	666
Esmeralda	Nevada	629
McPherson	Nebraska	623
Arthur	Nebraska	606
Alpine	California	484
King	Texas	464
Hinsdale	Colorado	202
Loving	Texas	164

Source: population statistics from the U.S. Bureau of the Census, U.S. Census of Population. 1970, Final Report PC(1) A1, 1971. Figures prepared by National Association of Counties, 1972.

Salaries of County Executives

County	Population*	Salary**	Population Rank	Salary Rank
Greater Anchorage Area Borough, Alaska	102,994	$ 21,000	35	37
North Star Borough, Alaska	30,618	28,022	39	21
Haines Borough, Alaska	1,351	360	46	44
Juneau City & Borough, Alaska	13,556	29,000	41	18
Kenai Peninsula Borough, Alaska	8,445	30,264	43	12
Ketchikan Gateway Borough, Alaska	10,041	18,500	42	39
Kodiak Island Borough, Alaska	6,357	6,750	44	42
North Slope Borough, Alaska	3,500		45	—
San Francisco, California	715,674	41,894	12	3
Denver, Colorado	514,678	27,500	21	22
New Castle County, Delaware	385,856	20,500	24	38
Dade County, Florida	1,267,792	6,000	3	43
Jacksonville and Duval County, Florida	528,865	30,000	20	13
Columbus-Muscogee County, Georgia	167,377	25,500	32	27

Hawaii County, Hawaii	63,468	36	11
Honolulu, Hawaii	629,176	15	9
Kauai County, Hawaii	29,761	40	19
Maui County, Hawaii	46,156	38	10
Cook County, Illinois	5,492,369	1	—
Indianapolis-Marion County, Indiana	792,299	11	36
Baton Rouge-East Baton Rouge Parish, Louisiana	285,167	27	33
Jefferson Parish, Louisiana	337,568	25	34
New Orleans, Louisiana	593,471	17	28
Anne Arundel Co., Maryland	297,539	26	23
Baltimore County, Maryland	621,077	16	14
City of Baltimore, Maryland	905,759	9	6
Howard County, Maryland	61,911	37	32
Montgomery County, Maryland	552,809	19	7
Prince George's County, Maryland	660,567	13	8
Jackson County, Missouri	654,558	14	29
St. Louis County, Missouri	951,353	8	30
Broome County, New York	221,815	30	24
Dutchess County, New York	222,295	29	26
Erie County, New York	1,113,491	6	5
Nassau County, New York	1,422,905	2	1
Oneida County, New York	273,037	28	35
Onondaga County, New York	472,185	22	15

County	Population*	Salary**		
Orange County, New York	220,558	30,000	31	16
Suffolk County, New York	1,116,672	36,490	5	4
Westchester County, New York	891,409	49,130	10	2
Multnomah County, Oregon	556,667	28,268	18	20
Nashville-Davidson County, Tennessee	448,003	25,000	23	31
King County, Washington	1,156,633	27,000	4	25
Milwaukee County, Wisconsin	1,054,063	30,000	7	17
Brown County, Wisconsin	158,244	17,500	33	41
Outagamie County, Wisconsin	119,356	18,500	34	40

*population figures based on 1970 Bureau of Census.
**salary figures based on 1972 NACO survey.

CONSOLIDATIONS

Mergers by Legislative Action - 9

New Orleans-Orleans Parish, Louisiana	1805
Boston - Suffolk County, Massachusetts	1821
Philadelphia - Philadelphia County, Pennsylvania	1854
San Francisco - San Francisco County, California	1856
New York - New York County, New York	1874
New York and Brooklyn - Queens and Richmond Counties, New York	1898
Honolulu - Honolulu County, Hawaii	1907
Denver - Denver County, Colorado	1904
Indianapolis - Marion County, Indiana	1969

Mergers by Referendum - 12

Baton Rouge - East Baton Rouge Parish, Louisiana	1947
Hampton - Elizabeth City County, Virginia	1952
Nashville - Davidson County, Tennessee (defeated in 1958)	1962
Virginia Beach - Princess Anne County, Virginia	1962
South Norfolk - Norfolk County, Virginia	1962
Jacksonville - Duval County, Florida (defeated in 1935)	1967
Juneau - Greater Juneau Borough, Alaska	1969
Carson City - Ormsby County, Nevada	1969
Columbus - Muscogee County, Georgia (defeated in 1962)	1970
Sitka - Greater Sitka Borough, Alaska	1971
Suffolk - Nansemond County, Virginia	1972
Lexington - Fayette County, Kentucky	1972

There seems to be no one universal definition for city-county consolidation. The National Association of Counties uses the following definition:

City-County Consolidation: A city-county consolidation or merger involves the unification of the governments of one or more cities with the surrounding county. As a result of the consolidation, the boundary lines of the jurisdictions involved become coterminous. However, certain incorporated jurisdictions may opt to be excluded from the consolidation.

231

Salaries for Fifteen County Government Positions

| Position | Counties 100,000 – 249,999 | | | | | |
	No. of Counties Responding 1968	No. of Counties Responding 1972	Highest Annual Salary 1968	Highest Annual Salary 1972	Average Annual Salary 1968	Average Annual Salary 1972
Clerk	54	88	18,000	24,470	10,539	13,932
Recorder	54	56	13,200	20,400	7,772	13,261
Auditor	54	61	16,500	25,800	10,648	14,777
Treasurer	54	95	18,000	25,103	10,787	14,463
Assessor	54	82	17,400	29,244	10,854	15,454
Director Public Works	54	34	20,000	29,680	15,068	20,741
Sheriff	54	111	17,400	25,800	11,084	15,437
Director Public Safety	54	10	13,525	26,532	8,306	14,550
Planning Director	54	74	17,160	25,800	10,805	16,456
Chief Personnel Officer	54	46	14,163	27,350	8,983	14,445
County Counsel	54	52	21,600	33,864	12,165	15,579
Health Director	54	70	28,000	40,536	16,263	23,499
Director Parks & Recreation	54	55	13,760	20,730	7,112	13,245
Superintendent of Schools	54	34	23,268	35,000	15,049	22,831
Director Public Welfare	54	63	17,280	29,100	10,618	16,543

Counties 250,000 – 499,999.

Clerk	29	38	17,997	23,174	13,248	15,769
Recorder	29	24	19,712	21,102	11,027	16,061
Auditor	29	28	19,200	23,940	13,036	16,733
Treasurer	29	42	23,744	31,384	13,816	15,847
Assessor	29	36	19,200	24,740	12,629	16,529
Director Public Works	29	19	27,488	32,388	16,656	23,109
Director Public Safety	29	9	9,492	20,500	9,137	14,151
Planning Director	29	32	19,416	27,300	14,668	18,730
Chief Personnel Officer	29	31	18,612	24,936	13,674	16,504
County Counsel	29	27	28,863	35,076	15,945	20,502
Health Director	29	23	27,996	38,000	18,312	28,268
Director Parks & Recreation	29	29	16,780	24,880	11,968	15,629
Superintendent of Schools	29	18	30,000	37,500	18,631	25,010
Director Public Welfare	29	19	21,540	28,680	15,194	19,976

Counties over 500,000

Clerk	35	35	21,288	37,500	16,351	21,835
Recorder	35	17	26,000	25,000	15,527	19,476
Auditor	35	29	24,075	32,630	17,554	23,332
Treasurer	35	36	23,500	33,500	17,104	21,671
Assessor	35	39	30,306	37,500	17,645	24,338
Director Public Works	35	33	31,496	38,500	20,987	29,383
Sheriff	35	39	26,160	33,372	17,500	24,591

Director Public Safety	35	9	20,500	33,280	14,635	22,787
Planning Director	35	34	29,256	32,100	17,920	23,844
Chief Personnel Officer	35	36	27,180	31,020	16,976	23,002
County Counsel	35	32	31,944	40,668	20,473	28,910
Health Director	35	32	32,680	44,000	23,796	33,618
Director Parks & Recreation	35	29	25,958	32,630	18,207	23,624
Superintendent of Schools	35	19	32,500	35,000	19,302	24,437
Director Public Welfare	35	26	29,460	39,510	20,146	26,513

State Associations of Counties

State Associations of Counties are found in 47 of the 48 states that have functional county governments. Operating at the state level, these organizations bolster the efforts of the National Association of Counties and over the years the working relationships between the national and state associations have been growing. Primary activities of the associations focus on monitoring and molding state legislation concerning county government, and serving as a source of information on all aspects of county government's operations. In several states there exist two organizations, one to represent county board members, another to serve as row officers.

Association of County
  Commissioners of Alabama
660 Adams Avenue
Montgomery, Alabama
  36104

Alaska Municipal League
204 N. Franklin
Juneau, Alaska 99801

Arizona Association of
  Counties
Adams Hotel, Suite 257
Phoenix, Arizona 85004

Association of Arkansas
  Counties
Lee County Courthouse
Marianna, Arkansas 72360

County Supervisors Association of California
11th and L. Building
Sacramento, California
  95814

Colorado State Association of
  County Commissioners
1500 Grant Street
Denver, Colorado 80203

Delaware State Association
  of Counties
Sussex County Courthouse
Georgetown, Delaware 19947

State Association of County
  Commissioners of Florida
P.O. Box 549
Tallahassee, Florida 32302

Association of County
Commissioners of Georgia
Suite 1120 Carnegie Bldg.
Atlanta, Georgia 30303

Hawaii State Association of
Counties
Room 307, City Hall
Honolulu, Hawaii 96813

Idaho Association of
Commissioners and Clerks
Latah County Courthouse
Moscow, Idaho

Illinois Association of Supervisors and County
Commissioners
415 Ridgely Building
Springfield, Illinois 62702

Association of Indiana
Counties
317 Illinois Building
17 West Market Street
Indianapolis, Indiana 46204

North Carolina Association
of County Commissioners
Wachovia Bank Building,
4th Floor
P.O. Box 1488
Raleigh, North Carolina
27602

North Dakota County
Commissioners
Stutsman County
Jamestown, North Dakota
58401

County Commissioners
Association of Ohio
41 S. High Street
Neil House, M-58
Columbus, Ohio 43215

Oklahoma County
Commissioners Association
Washington County
Courthouse
Cordell, Oklahoma

Association of Oregon
Counties
P.O. Box 2051
Salem, Oregon 97308

Pennsylvania State
Association of County
Commissioners
301 Blackstone Building
112 Market Street
Harrisburg, Pennsylvania
17101

South Carolina Association
of Counties
1227 Main Street
808 SCN Center
Columbia, South Carolina
29201

South Dakota Association of
County Commissioners
Turner County Courthouse
Parker, South Dakota 57053

Tennessee County Services
Association
226 Capital Blvd. Building
Nashville, Tennessee 37219

County Judges &
Commissioners Association
of Texas
P.O. Box 6144
Longview, Texas

Texas Association of
Counties
P.O. Box 6144
Longview, Texas 75601

Utah Association of Counties
10 Broadway Building
10 W. Broadway, Suite 315
Salt Lake City, Utah 84101

Virginia Association of
Counties
402 County Office Building
Charlottesville, Virginia
22901

Washington State
Association of Counties
106 Maple Park
Olympia, Washington 98501

Washington State
Association of Elected
County Officials

Room 205
Capital Park Building
1063 Capitol Way
Olympia, Washington 98501

West Virginia Association
of County Officials
207½ Duffy Street
Charleston, West Virginia
25339

Wisconsin County Boards
Association
229 Monona Avenue,
Suite 516
Madison, Wisconsin 53703

Wyoming County
Commissioners' Association
P.O. Box 3321
University Station
Laramie, Wyoming 82070

Wyoming Association of
County Officials
Park County Courthouse
Cody, Wyoming 82414

Index

Adams County,
Pennsylvania, 47
Advisory Commission on
Intergovernmental
Relations, 14-15, 51, 55,
58, 184, 189
Agnew, Spiro T., 18, 97
Alameda County,
California, 102
Allegheny County,
Pennsylvania, 31, 142
American Federation of
State, County and
Municipal Employees,
111, 114, 117, 120, 132
Apportionment.
See Reapportionment
Arlington County,
Virginia, 99
Assembly of
Governmental
Employees, 120
Assessment, 40-41, 84-86;
See also Property taxes

Association of Bay Area
Governments, 154

Baltimore County,
Maryland, 88, 89, 97
Baton Rouge-East Baton
Rouge Parish,
Louisiana, 163, 179, 186
Bibb County, Georgia, 162
Black Jack, Missouri,
64-65
Bradley, Thomas, 206

Charleston County, South
Carolina, 112-113, 124,
126
Chatham County, Georgia,
23
Citizens' associations, 53,
60-62
City-county consolidation,
162-167, 199
City-county
reorganization, 156-167,
199

239

241